The MBA Bubble

Why Getting an MBA Degree Is a Bad Idea

Mariana Zanetti

www.thembabubble.com

Copyright © 2013 by Mariana Zanetti

All rights reserved

ISBN 978-1490942933

To Gastón and Mathias, who are the light in my life.

To my mother, to my Argentine family, to my Spanish family, and to my French family, for their help and unconditional support in this project.

Table of Contents

Why I Wrote This Book 7

How to Read This Book 17

A Basic Mistake in Logic 29

Any Investment in Education Is Good… Isn't It? 37

MBAs Are Cholesterol Free 51

The Rankings: Bait for the Naïve 65

Selling One's Soul to the Devil 75

If You Want to Be Rich, Don't Get an MBA 89

Why There Is So Little Criticism of the MBA 101

Why Do Business Schools Still Have Customers? 111

The Magic Moment when You Forgot That You Are the Customer 119

Recognize Your Professional Goals First 131

The MBA and the Employability Myth 143

If You Didn't Go to Business School, You Don't Know Them 155

If You Didn't Learn It in Business School, You Don't Know It 163

5

A Unique and Incomparable Experience...Isn't It? 175

The Master of the Universe 181

Is It Possible to Have an MBA and Have a Sense of Ethics? 189

The Exceptions to the Rule 195

My Story 205

Acknowledgments 219

1
Why I Wrote This Book

There are only two rules for writing:
To have something to say and to say it.

Oscar Wilde

I admit it. To advise someone to give up pursuing a master of business administration (MBA) degree is kind of a provocation because an MBA degree, especially one from a top business school, is supposed to be a ticket to professional success. So that's it—I am going to do something provocative. Throughout this book, I am going to show you why pursuing an MBA is a very bad decision and a ruinous investment. In fact, it is not even an investment; it is a waste of money—lots of money. So if you don't want to do something insane with your savings or to mortgage your life into monumental debt, I recommend that you continue reading.

Nevertheless, I do not question the quality of the education one derives in an MBA program. I do not question the professors' knowledge. I will not say that employers do not value MBAs. Or that it is not a fantastic experience. Or that you won't meet wonderful and interesting people in the MBA program. Not at all.

The MBA Bubble

Instead, I will present some common beliefs about MBAs that are true:

- The professors are brilliant (with a few exceptions). They know their subjects, they know how to teach, and they prepare brilliantly for their classes.

- An MBA looks really good on someone's résumé. Most employers value the degree.

- Most students value the MBA experience.

- Many studies show that wages of MBA graduates are significantly higher than those of non-MBAs.

- The network one develops during an MBA program is a valuable asset.

- MBA graduates have a higher probability of occupying a management position than non-MBAs.

Why does this book contradict itself from the very beginning? How can an MBA be a ruinous investment if the preceding statements are true?

Let's go step by step. First of all, let me tell you about my own experience. Unlike many authors who write books about the MBA, I do have the degree. And as an

Why I Wrote This Book

aggravating factor, I have an MBA degree from a top-ranked European business school. Almost without exception, it appears on the lists of top European schools with the most prestigious rankings. I did not go to Harvard, Wharton, Stanford, or any of the other top-tier American schools. I didn't even try to get in. That is fortunate for me because if I had been admitted, I would have multiplied my ruin by three. In fact, it was a Harvard MBA who helped me with my application to business school. The vision of Harvard Business School that he transmitted to me did not change my mind on this issue, though.

The business school from which I obtained my MBA is not a secret, but it is not relevant for the arguments of this book, either. So if you want to know which school it is, you can check it out easily. Some business schools are considered better than mine, and many schools are considered worse. Regardless of the school, the MBA programs' cost is proportional to this perception. The facts I expose in this book are valid regardless of the brand of the business school itself. I do not question the "manufacturer" or the brand, but the value added by the "product."

I obtained my degree ten years ago. Most of the ideas that you are going to read in this book come from the very first months of the program. Neither the experiences I had after I graduated nor the economic crisis have changed my opinion—if anything, they have accentuated it.

The MBA Bubble

This may sound confusing. But before clarifying the topic, let me confuse you even more: *I have met all the professional goals I set for myself when I was pursuing my MBA.* In addition, I met wonderful and brilliant people with whom I am still in contact. And as if this was not enough to confuse you, many of the classes I attended left me open-mouthed with wonder. I had access to brilliant professors and learned many interesting things.

Do you see what is missing in the facts I have just mentioned? Don't worry. I did not see what was missing, either, and I fell into the trap. I came fast to the conclusion most people do when seeing this information: *Getting an MBA will have a positive impact on your career, help you meet your professional goals, and increase your income and employability. With an MBA, your career will become more satisfactory and prosperous.*

That is a damned wrong conclusion!

I am not going to tell you that the information you have about MBAs is not true. *I am, however, going to question the conclusions that you are taking from that information.*

A few months after beginning my MBA, I realized I had committed *one of the worst mistakes of my life.* I had two choices: I could quit the program, give up my chance of getting the diploma, and lose my tuition fees,

Why I Wrote This Book

or I could continue moving forward and continue the most ridiculous race of all.

I remember one day during the program, I was out of my mind with frustration. At the edge of depression, I fired my ire in a very direct way at the director of the program. I reproached the nonsense of the monumental personal and financial effort we students were expending. Her response was rapid: "You applied to the wrong program." My frustration did not disturb her at all.

She was right. I had made an enormous mistake. Her answer turned around in my head for years. How was it possible that I had made such a huge mistake? Simple—I did not have enough information to make my decision properly. But how could it possibly be that this information was not available? Simple—No one had a vested interest in making this information available to potential enrollees.

Not all MBA graduates share my opinion or consider their MBA to be a mistake. However, a fair percentage of them have seen how the MBA has been a negative influence in their lives, or a big disappointment.

That's why I wrote this book. What you are going to read here is information you probably won't read anywhere else. It is in no one's best interest to reveal this truth to you. But you need to know it before you mortgage your life with an extremely poor and costly decision that is difficult to turn back from once you pay your first tuition bill.

I only wish someone else had written a book like this before I entered my MBA program so that I could have read it and avoided the costly mistake that pulled me away from my goals. A book like this would have helped many of my colleagues from spending their savings senselessly or carrying monumental debt that burdened them for years.

I have written the book that would have saved me valuable time. I have written the book that would have showed many MBA graduates that they could have had the same professional results without being "victims" of business schools' marketing. I have written it for young, ambitious professionals like you who have a few years of professional experience. Please read this book so that you can make a more informed decision about entering an MBA program.

I do not mean that an MBA has no benefits, but what you get in return for it is not worth the enormous financial, personal, and opportunity costs that are not compensated by the value an MBA degree provides.

I have been sure of this for ten years. The world has changed very much since then, making my thoughts even more radical:

- The cost of access to knowledge has decreased significantly with new technologies.

- Contacting great and brilliant people has never been so easy or so free. Through social networks, you do not even have to spend money on a phone call.

- The cost of MBA tuition has increased dramatically, but the added value of the program has decreased drastically to almost zero. There is an education bubble that is about to burst.

- MBA programs were conceived to help people face the challenges of the Industrial Age. The West has left this age behind and has been in the Information Age for decades now.

Is it clearer to you? Not yet? Let me tell you an anecdote that confirmed the nonsense of my getting the degree. A few years after getting my MBA, I was in a meeting with a brilliant manager. I admired him. He was a smart person. He read a lot and engaged in some astute discussions with his colleagues on the board on which he served. In my opinion, he was superior to the others because he was one of the most respected people in the company and because of his path in the company. It was evident to me that many directors had an MBA, so I figured he would surely have one also. One day I asked him if he had an MBA. His response was "Me, an MBA? Listen, I try not to make stupid decisions in my life."

That was the way I was feeling with my nice blue-lettered degree and my debt: stupid enough. I could have met exactly the same goals in my professional career without spending my savings and my family's on the noble cause of business-school profitability.

Of course, if this director had had an MBA, the business school would have taken the credit for his achievements.

Do not misinterpret me. I do not want the business-school industry to sink, nor do I seek "revenge" for my mistake. I am the only one to blame because it was my mistake. They didn't put a gun in my head to apply. But I would like you to avoid making the same mistake I did.

In fact, I dream that society will find a way of benefiting from such a temple of brilliant talent because it is of such little value.

If business schools do not change their value proposition, it is because there is still a huge demand for them, so they do not have any incentive to change. But what would happen if their enrollment declined? Well, it is already happening; the bubble is about to burst. Don't let it find you unaware and unprepared.

If you already have an MBA, believe me, I am very sorry. There is a high probability that it has been a ruinous investment for you (though there are exceptions, and I hope from the bottom of my heart that your case is one of them). I can say to you in any case that I share your feelings because we share the same

Why I Wrote This Book

wrong decision. If you are an MBA student, I am very sorry also. You don't have a way back; it is too late to reverse your decision. But you can try to minimize the damage by reading this book.

Before getting mad at me for "devaluating" your degree, let me tell you what I am not going to say in this book: I am not going to say that you are not going to be successful. I am not going to say that you are stupid. I am not going to say that you do not belong in an elite group. Instead I will show you that the MBA is not the cause of your success but the consequence of who you already are. You never needed the MBA to succeed.

If you always wanted to have an MBA but could not get it for some reason, know that destiny has given you an unexpected gift. By the time you have read this book, your regrets will have faded away and you will look at your MBA colleagues with sorrow for what they have been through uselessly.

If you are planning to get an MBA, please read with attention. This book can prevent you from making one of the worst financial and personal decisions of your life. Even if you are unemployed and you think that it is a good time to follow the program, it is possible that you will never be able to pay the money back, and certainly you will never get your time back. There are much more profitable options for reaching your goals. And I will go even further: It is possible that the MBA will turn your life into a nightmare, though you may not realize it right now.

The MBA Bubble

You may be thinking, *What about all the information about MBA degrees resulting in high wages, top management positions, employers' appreciation, and valuable networking opportunities?*

Please continue reading. I will explain it all.

2
How to Read This Book

I don't understand why people are frightened of new ideas; I am frightened of the old ones.

John Cage, American Composer

Imagine that we are in the year 2006, in Spain. Imagine that you and I are two colleagues, discussing our lives at the coffee machine. You tell me that you are finally going to buy your own house. You have been saving for four years, and you don't want to wait any longer. You don't want to continue throwing your money away every month by renting.

Suddenly, something unexpected happens: I advise you not to buy. I tell you that it would be better to continue renting your house, that to buy a house at this moment is a terrible decision. Wow. You hesitate, trying to decide whether to change the topic of discussion or hear me out. You choose the second option.

So I begin my monologue. I say that I am in touch with people in the real estate business. I say that they told me that real estate prices are inflated by a bubble effect. In other words, homes are priced at least 30 percent higher than they are worth. In addition, I say that the Spanish economic model is a model of risk because there are not enough alternative sources of growth. I say that if this is combined with a global crisis (still confessing that in 2006, I would never have imagined the magnitude of the 2008 crisis), unemployment in Spain could increase several points. Your risk of losing your job and not being able to make your house payments is high. Besides, in Spain, you cannot return your house keys to the bank and walk away like you can in the United States, so you risk losing your job and your house and having eternal debt without getting anything in return.

Now imagine that we are in 2012. You lost your job in 2011, but fortunately you found another. The only problem is that you are earning 30 percent less, and you work infinite hours on the other side of the city. You have a three-hour commute every day. You never receive a bonus because sales are low. Your house is worth less today than the loan that finances it. The monthly payments are asphyxiating you, and you are afraid of losing your job at any time. You are enslaved.

Well, I will not make you suffer any more. The exercises of imagination are over. Nevertheless, this story could be true.

You are probably wondering what this has to do with the MBA. Well, the story has nothing to do with it. But the way of thinking has everything to do with it.

In this book, I present an argument that is not common, just as it was not common in Spain in 2006 for people to say that buying a house was a bad idea. But as the

How to Read this Book

Spanish author Raimón Samsó says, do not confuse the frequent thing with the normal thing. It is not normal for people to believe that it is necessary to pay a fortune and to spend one or two years of their lives to obtain practically the same results as if they didn't. It is just not normal.

The Good Skepticism

I am not going to ask you to believe everything I say. But if you are to take advantage of this book, you should read it and allow yourself to be a skeptic in a good way.

There are two ways of being a sceptic. The first one, the most frequent, is the wrong way. You hear an argument that goes against the tide and defies your beliefs and mental models, and you discount it. For example, you hear an argument stating that it is possible to earn more by working less. And you think *Yeah, sure...you wish*. And you just forget it. But what if it were possible? Well, you will never know. The second way to be a skeptic is the good way, the most normal. With this way of thinking, you say, in response to the above argument, "It sounds strange; it does not seem to be possible. But what consequences would it have for me if it were true? It would probably be worth it to analyze it."

I have always been a skeptic in the good way, but as for the MBA, I did not have the chance. At that time, nobody was proclaiming yet that getting the degree was a bad idea. Today you are lucky to have this possibility.

19

Do not waste it. Consider this notion and analyze your decision deeply.

Many things have changed today since then, and the voices that question the value of the MBA are increasingly common, though not enough yet to change the system. These voices come also from people like me who regret their decision, even if their degree is from one of the most prestigious business schools in the world.

Challenging Mental Models

A mental model is a description of how the world works. We all have mental models because they facilitate life. I have a mental model that states that when I ask for things nicely, with a "please," people are much more likely to comply with my request. For years, this mental model worked fantastically for me, and until now, I have never had to review it. Nevertheless, I have had to review some others. For example, when I was a child, I had a mental model stating that speaking to strangers was dangerous. But when I grew up, this model was not useful to me anymore because speaking to strangers is a great source of opportunity.

In 2006 in Spain, the majority of the population shared some mental models. One such mental model was the one asserting that real estate investments are profitable and riskless and that houses do not lose value over time. In view of the situation in 2013, it is obvious that these

How to Read this Book

mental models were erroneous and should have been reviewed more carefully.

So that you can take the arguments of this book into consideration, the first thing I am going to ask you to do is to be open to reviewing your mental models. I am not asking you to give them up, but I will ask you to be open to analyzing them.

Reviewing your mental models and making them more accurate will give you spectacular results in your life. Frequently, when you identify your mental model, you realize that you can reach your goals in a much more efficient way. On the contrary, a vague or incorrect mental model can have disastrous consequences in your life.

Do you identify some of the following mental models as yours?

- A person's level of education has a positive correlation with his or her employability and income. Therefore, any educational investment has a positive return on investment (ROI).

- A stable and high-paying job with a big company is essential to prosperity and economic stability.

- An MBA (especially from a top business school) opens doors for the best jobs.

… The MBA Bubble

- If MBA graduates' wages are at least 35 percent higher than those of non-MBAs, the MBA degree is a good investment.

- If getting an MBA were a bad idea, business schools would not have enough students to justify their existence.

- If the increase of post-MBA wages is 50 percent compared to pre-MBA wages, a positive ROI is perceived in the short term.

- An MBA is an indispensable tool for progressing to top management positions.

I will say that those are *all* imprecise mental models, and some of them are completely incorrect.

I will explain it to you in detail throughout the book. But first, I am going to invite you to question the basis of your worldview.

The Industrial Age Is Dead

The first thing I will question is your belief that we are still living in the Industrial Age. I do not blame you if you were educated during that time period. Our parents grew up in that time period. I did not, and you may not have. I invite you to see on YouTube a speech delivered by Sir Ken Robinson[1] about how the paradigms of

How to Read this Book

education are changing. It is brilliant; please don't miss it.

In the Industrial Age, a college degree was a guarantee to obtain a good job. Nowadays, when we cannot predict what is going to happen with the economy next week, having a degree can be nice, but it is no longer a guarantee.

The MBA is not even as valuable as a bachelor's degree. It is not necessary to exercise managerial functions. If you still think you need an MBA degree to access certain positions, I will invite you later to be a skeptic in the good way regarding this belief. An MBA is not a guarantee of success at all.

"I think [the MBAs] are sort of a joke. Unless you want to be a doctor, a lawyer, or an engineer, why do you really need something beyond a bachelor's? Do you not have enough debt as it is?" the writer David Wolinski affirms.[2] I can tell that the author has been lucky to remain immune to the virus of business schools' marketing. He sees that his MBA colleagues feel adrift with their careers. In fact, he is surprised that this continues being discussed nowadays and that it is not evident to the whole world. But it is not evident, and that's why I wrote this book. According to Wolinski, the MBA degree was created in a time when the world worked in another way. He thinks the programs are a waste of time and money. You see, I am not the only one.

The MBA Bubble

The history of the MBA shows that its value proposition is completely out of date with the reality of today's world. Business schools still continue looking for what worked in the past and do not have any incentive to design a program that aligns with the future.

The first MBA was born in 1881 with the Wharton Business School at the University of Pennsylvania. Its aim? To analyze the challenges of the nascent Industrial Age, bringing together the directors of the most prosperous industrial companies to share their knowledge with students. Dartmouth and Harvard followed Wharton at the beginning of the twentieth century—yes, you read that correctly—at the beginning of the last century. I guess that you think that after all these years, the schools updated their programs or teaching methods to adapt them to the challenges of the unpredictable environment of the twenty-first century...well, not really. The case method, adopted by most business schools, was born in 1924 at Harvard and continues basically the same since then. What is it based on? Analysis of a real business case to contribute solutions.... Or, in other words, *analyzing the past and hoping it will serve to control the situations of the future.*

But the world does not work this way anymore, I am sorry to give you this news. Neither in communities nor in business, the past is no longer a reference to understand the future. That's why the twenty-first century gurus speak about Lean methodologies, which in street language would sound more or less like this:

How to Read this Book

"Make a hypothesis today. Tomorrow, create a minimal viable product. The day after tomorrow, put it on the market and see what happens in a few days. If it has sold, then improve your version and grow. If it has not, start over again." Very effective and simple. That's why business schools do not teach it. It is not a business for them.

Do you live in a world that does not exist any longer? This is what Raimón Samsó will ask you in his book[3] (sorry, it is not translated into English, but it surely will be soon). The Industrial Age is dead. We are living now in the Information Age, in which the information is abundant and accessible. To create wealth in the west side of the world, it is not necessary to have neither working capital nor land. Now it is possible to create wealth with valuable information and with talent, whereas the MBA will teach you what brilliant teachers learned during some past decades about how to manage an industrial company. There is nothing wrong with that if you dream of living in China. In fact, more and more business schools are opening headquarters in Asia, which seems more than interesting.

People are discussing this. In a post of his blog in the Spanish newspaper *CincoDías*, the journalist and MBA Juan Luis Manfredi recommends that you should consider getting your MBA in Asia. What is his point? That the world has changed.

The labor paradigm of the Industrial Age damaged us, especially the idea of that we will work as madmen up to retiring at the age of sixty-five. If you embrace this paradigm, it may seem to you that the MBA has certain logic in your plans: You will run faster for fifteen to twenty years. You will pay back your investment in a few years, and then you will amass a small fortune that will allow you to retire as soon as possible so that you can finally enjoy life. You hope that the future will be that predictable, as it was in the Industrial Age. In addition, you think that working 100 hours per week for years at jobs that make you miserable is a fair price to pay.

Well, it is not. Remove retirement from the equation because the most probable scenario is that by the time you retire, the government will have advanced the retirement age to seventy-five 75. And if you keep the stressful 100-hour-per-week lifestyle, you will not live past fifty. You also will live in constant insecurity because this is a reality of our time. Job security is dead, and the MBA will not change that. Corporate careers do not last beyond the age of forty-five or fifty. Do you want me to tell you the stories I know from MBA graduates who lost their jobs in 2008? When they calculated the MBA ROI, they considered a predictable future, but it did not play out that way.

Do you still find any logic in investing tens or even hundreds of thousands of dollars on a degree when you don't know how the world will be like in even two years? Does it still seem to be a safe investment to you only because it is an educational investment?

If you do not buy this argument yet, it's OK. But I will ask you again to be a skeptic in the good way.

How to Read this Book

If you are employed with a big company, what is the percentage of employees older than forty-five (which means that they have at least twenty years of work life ahead)? Does it fit with the percentage of the general population in this age range? Do you know of a company in which this percentage is representative? I would argue that public companies are not representative. I predict that the stability of employment in the public sector will deteriorate in future years.

In an article in *The Economist*, Philip Delves Broughton, a Harvard MBA and author of *Ahead of the Curve* (outside the US it's tittled *What They Teach You at Harvard Business School*), contends that corporate life does not last beyond the age of forty-something or fifty. He also questions the ethics of business schools' value proposition[4], offering products for astronomical amounts of money that students will not be able to pay back before their forties.

If you feel nostalgic for the Industrial Age and you believe that buying an MBA will help you extend your viability in the workplace, you will be a victim of business schools' marketing. You will buy the illusion that a nice piece of paper will give you the opportunity to live in this world that no longer exists.

Sorry to disappoint you. In my professional career, I have seen many managers (with or without an MBA) going through situations they were not prepared for. They were not prepared to lose their jobs at age forty-five. They were not prepared not to retire from the company in which they worked their hands off for years. They were not prepared for the end of the Industrial Age.

I recommend you to prepare yourself, but the MBA is not the best way to do it.

You may be thinking that even though the world is unstable, you still need to find a job, and everything indicates that the MBA will improve your options, whatever they are or will be.

But be careful. Maybe you are making a *basic mistake in logic*.

3
A Basic Mistake in Logic

The logic now in use serves rather to fix and give stability to the errors which have their foundation in commonly received notions than to help the search for truth.

Sir Francis Bacon, English Philosopher and Statesman

Let me please take it for granted that if you aspire to complete an MBA degree, it means you have enough connections between your neurons. Otherwise, they would not admit you. So I take it for granted.

Therefore, I will suppose that you don't mind making a couple of logical exercises with me, right? Here we go.

Given that A is greater than B and that B is greater than C, can I affirm that A is greater than C? Yes, of course. Well done.

Let's complicate the thing a little bit. Suppose I have three chests, and one of them contains a treasure. Only one of three of the following legends is true. Where is the treasure?

Legend of Chest 1: The treasure is not in Chest 2.

The MBA Bubble

Legend of Chest 2: The treasure is here.

Legend of Chest 3: The treasure is not here.

I hope you could find the right answer because finding the treasure depends on it.

I especially hope you will be able to solve the next exercise because, in fact, if you get the wrong answer, you risk much, much more than losing an imaginary treasure:

MBA graduates earn significantly more than non-MBAs. Assuming that this differential compensates the costs of the program, the MBA is a good investment.

True or false? What do you say?

I am going to tell you what I answered at one time. I said it was true. In fact, there are studies that demonstrate statistically the first part of the phrase[5], so it is not in doubt. In any case, I assumed that an MBA was a good investment.

Now tell me what you think about the following conclusion:

Studies of consumption realized by Ferrari demonstrate that 90 percent of Ferrari's owners are millionaires. In view of these results, to buy a Ferrari is a good

A Basic Mistake in Logic

investment because it drastically increases the probability of turning into a millionaire.

How about that? Would you sell your house to buy a Ferrari so that you would have a higher probability of being a millionaire? Do you consider it to be a good investment?

No, it is not. I would not do it. But the previous statement and the preceding one share the same mistake in logic. Have you discovered what it is?

Correlation is not equal to causality.

I repeat: *Correlation is not equal to causality*. The first part in each statement talks about a correlation between two facts. The second part assumes that one of the facts is the cause of the other one. But to assume that, it is necessary to demonstrate more things.

I guess you will say to me that it is obvious that the reason for the salary increase is the MBA.

OK. I will admit that it seems obvious. But you should admit that from a logical point of view, causality is not proved by enunciating correlation. Do you follow me?

And why does it seem obvious to you that the cause of the salary increase is the MBA? Because you assume, I guess, that any investment in "formal" education is safe

31

and that a correlation between these facts only confirms your mental model.

So let me question your mental model in a more direct way. Though correlation is not equal to causality, the opposite does work: *The absence of correlation rejects causality.*

A devastating study of the Academy of Management, Learning and Education (AMLE) led by Stanford professor Jeffrey Pfeffer demonstrates that *there is no correlation between an MBA and professional success, including salary*[6]. However, Pfeffer has no doubts about business schools being a great business. What do you think about this?

The MBA does not have a causality rapport with professional success, as also shown by another study carried out by *BusinessWeek.*[7]

But maybe you still do not understand it. I don't blame you. I made the same mistake in logic. How could be there a correlation between higher wages and an MBA but not between an MBA and professional success?

The fact is that success is more frequent among MBA graduates than it is in the general population of graduates with bachelor's degrees. But among successful people, the MBA is not more frequent than non-MBAs. Do you see it? From a logical point of view, it is like affirming that the most frequent thing is that those who own a Ferrari are millionaires, but

A Basic Mistake in Logic

among the millionaires, the most frequent thing is to have a Porsche. Does this start to make sense?

Let me say first how I started to understand this terrible mistake in logic. When I realized my mistake, I squandered any hope of seeing my MBA as a good decision in the long term.

In my first corporate job after completing my MBA, the degree was a not even a requirement (in fact, it is not a requirement most of the time[8]). Most people in the same position did not have it. Of course my employer valued it. But the condition for which they offered me the job was my previous work experience.

One day by mistake, an employee of the Human Resources department sent a file to everybody containing the wages of the entire work force, from the CEO to store salespeople. Poor girl—it was a simple mistake to make, and it cost her her job. Anyway, mine was the second-lowest salary of the twenty-five-person product-management team. Ouch.

Nevertheless, there were some possible explanations for my low salary, such as the fact that I was coming from another country or sector. I never placed much importance on this.

Three years later and after two significant salary increases, a head hunter recruited me to work for the competition. My salary increased by 55 percent. Finally, my MBA was profitable! I was already earning over the average of my MBA classmates (at least over the average of those whose salaries I knew)...unless I had exactly the same salary as my new colleagues did, only one of whom had an MBA.

My conclusion is that *my MBA did not have any influence in my professional results*, neither in the good ones nor in the bad ones. What my employers valued most were my experience and my knowledge. When my salary increased so drastically, it was not because of the MBA but because of my strategic sectorial knowledge and my several years of experience.

To complete an MBA, you must pass through a demanding admission process—the more demanding, the more prestigious (and expensive) the school. And admission criteria correlate with professional success. Those who evaluate candidates' applications look for interesting previous experience, good-quality gray matter under the hair, ambition, and good recommendations from important people. All of these factors also correlate with higher wages, and my conclusion is that they are the real impetus for higher salaries.

If you have an MBA, you belong to the universe of those with graduate degrees who have a higher probability of being successful. The MBA did not give you that; you already had it before entering. And when you analyze this universe, the MBA only is a nice decoration on your résumé. It does not have any correlation with your success.

A Basic Mistake in Logic

You may be wondering if your salary will increase after completing an MBA degree. In my case, my salary decreased by 15 percent. The MBA is not to blame. I was unemployed in the middle of a depressed market, and I inserted myself into a different labor market in a different country.

Nevertheless, often salary does increase after graduation. In an article in the Spanish journal *CincoDías*, a German student at a "top" MBA program in Spain confesses that, although his revenue increased after graduation, it would have happened anyway due to the natural evolution of his career[9]. Again, the MBA was not the reason; it is obvious that careers have a natural evolution.

The AMLE study[10] also suggests that an MBA does not have any influence in helping people avoid professional failures such as the one experienced by Enron, a company that was led by a Harvard MBA.

It is so obvious that I can't understand how I could not see it before. And I am persuaded that business schools are perfectly aware that they add little value to students. But while many people are ready to pay a fortune to believe they do, nothing is going to change. It is such a good business!

The studies you will see on the value added by an MBA will only show correlation between facts, but it is in your own interest to analyze the causality. A *Forbes* article published in 2009, "The Great College Hoax,"

The MBA Bubble

warns against the common mistake of confusing correlation with causality regarding education investment. It also affirms that the way educational institutions sell their products is tinged with consumer fraud. But why do brilliant people mortgage their lives without analyzing their decision more deeply? Because of the education industrial complex that has cultivated the image of a degree as a sure investment.[11] Let me invite you to think more about whether it is indeed a good investment.

4
Any Investment in Education Is Good... Isn't It?

How is it that little children are so intelligent and men so stupid? It must be education that does it.

Alexandre Dumas

If you think that higher levels of education lead to higher income and a better socioeconomic position, let me say that I completely agree with you. On this, we share a mental model. I am persuaded that the more educated a person is, the more prosperous her life will be.

But if you think that the more diplomas you have on your résumé, the more prosperous you will be, then you and I begin to walk along different paths. That being said, I should admit that I have always been an obedient disciple of good academic performance: I was a flag bearer in high school (meaning that I had the best marks), I was at the head of my class in college, and I have a pretty nice MBA diploma from a "top" business school (beautiful diploma—seriously, you should see it!).

I would trade all of my credentials for the knowledge and education of a few successful entrepreneurs and investors. They are masters of their time and their lives. Many of them do not have any diplomas at all.

You may think that not everyone is born to be an entrepreneur and that most people need to get prepared to get a job. And though it is a topic about which I am passionate, it is not a debate for this book...for the moment.

You and I probably will agree that educational ROI must be analyzed, just as any other type of investment.

What most MBA applicants do is estimate the wages they will have after graduation and calculate how long it will take to earn the amount of money the degree costs. They take for granted the fact that they may get a six-figure job if they are applying for a top-tier position. The most advanced will realize that they should take into account lost wages if they are planning to pursue an MBA full time. If they are even more advanced, they can consider some notion of a discount rate (the value of money through time). And here you are with the result: *The MBA is paid back in a few years.* It is a great investment. It is a sure value on your résumé that will add additional income for life. Who would doubt the wisdom of plunging into an MBA program?

OK. Let me look for the finance notes I took in the MBA program. Here they are. Lesson number one: An investment should be evaluated only in contrast with its alternative.

Any Investment in Education Is Good... Isn't It?

"An investment should be evaluated only in contrast with its alternative"

Do you know how much I had to pay to learn that? Gosh! I should probably increase the price of this book!

Let's pretend that previous chapter never existed because it states that investing in an MBA degree typically generates the same results as not investing in one. So the differential is zero, in which case this chapter would end here. An MBA would be a ruinous investment. Or maybe that even if you read it carefully, you never bought my point about an MBA not being the cause of any wage increase. Maybe you think that the Stanford professor's study is not realistic or representative and that it shows tendentious results. Maybe you think that if this study were correct, business schools would not continue attracting students.

Just for the moment, let's suppose that getting an MBA is the only alternative you have, although that is far from being true. Just for the moment, I will not consider the most effective and profitable alternatives for you to reach your professional goals.

Finance Knowledge That Is Worth More than an MBA

There is a high probability that you do not have the essential skills needed to analyze your investment. When I analyzed mine, I didn't have them, nor did most of my MBA classmates. And believe me—most people in their twenties going to Harvard, Wharton, or Stanford do not have them, either.

I am not talking about the financial skills you learn in an MBA program. That information is about a lot of endless spreadsheets full of equations that mostly serve to stimulate the finance professor intellectually.

I am talking about personal finance, that knowledge that has the power to turn you into a prosperous person. Has someone already recommended to you a book on personal finance? The few dollars you can invest in this kind of book will be much more profitable than the tens or even hundreds of thousands of dollars you would spend on an MBA degree. When you read them, you will learn the basis for the development of your financial intelligence. None of them will recommend that you go to business school.

An MBA degree is not conceived to make you rich but to make rich the shareholders of business schools. The financial management you will learn there is conceived to control the financial flow in big corporations. They do not teach you to make financial decisions that serve you.

So if you don't mind, I am going to share a couple of basic concepts of personal finance, in case you do not know them. You may be surprised at the number of people who do not know these concepts because they are not taught at school.

Any Investment in Education Is Good... Isn't It?

Excuse me for beginning with such a basic and trivial concept. But even if you already know it, I am really surprised about the number of people who apply to MBA programs without knowing it.

Let's start with the difference between assets and liabilities. Assets put money in your pocket. Liabilities extract it. Assets will make your financial situation improve; liabilities will worsen it. For example, a house of your own that you rent to others is an asset because it generates profitability, but a house financed through a loan you have to pay is a liability. How would you qualify the MBA—asset or liability?

You will probably say an MBA is an asset because it will allow you to increase your income. Nevertheless, if you do not go to work after completing an MBA, it generates no income. So the MBA itself is not an asset. It is a liability. And it is a big one. If things do not go as you expected, you will not be able to sell it to recover part of your investment like you can do with some assets.

But if you insist, I invite you to evaluate the capacity of this liability to increase your income through your work.

Do you know how taxes work? You do not pay a percentage of your earnings. You pay several percentages according to the tax bracket of your income. These brackets depend on the country, but all the countries have basically the same principle. That means that for the first X dollars you earn, you pay, for example, 10 percent. For the following Y, 15 percent; for the following Z, 20 percent...*and it continues this way until the government takes almost half of every incremental dollar you earn*. Do you follow me? For example, in Spain in 2013, everything you earn over 53,407 € (~ $ 69,000) pays a 47 percent tax and can reach 52 percent for top brackets. In the United States, you pay much higher health insurance fees than in Europe, but a lower tax, which is approximately one-third of what you earn in the starting salary ranges of those who have MBA degrees, and it can go up to 39.6 percent.

So if you think that having an MBA will increase your salary by 50 percent (Didn't I persuade you in the previous chapter that this is not true?), indeed *what will come to your pocket is only two-thirds of it* if you work in the United States or half of it if you work in countries with higher taxes, such as Spain. That means only a 33 percent increase in the United States or 26 percent in Spain, for example.

This is what you must consider when calculating the return on your investment—the incremental income only. In addition, do not forget that you would not have a static career if you had not gotten an MBA. Your salary would have increased anyway as a consequence of your career's natural evolution. You would have more experience and would be able to do better work if you simply continued working during those two years you were in school. So I propose to remain with a more reasonable differential increase of around 35 percent.

Any Investment in Education Is Good... Isn't It?

That leads to a 23 percent net salary increase including tax in the United States or a 16 percent net increase including tax in Spain. In fact, 35 percent is the average gross salary increase MBA applicants usually think they will receive upon completing the degree.

In addition, you should calculate the value of the money you spend on the MBA program over time, including the risk of not finding a good job immediately and of not fulfilling your salary expectations. In other words, you will have to calculate the net present value (NPV) of your investment.

I am going to tell you a secret. If you type "How to calculate NPV and IRR (internal rate of return)" in Google, you will probably find free tutorials that show you how to do it. Excel's "Help" feature also explains it. But if you ask the admissions personnel of the business school, they will say to you that you have to pay tuition to learn this information.

If you do not want to calculate it yourself, do not worry. Others have done it for you already.

Christian Schraga, a graduate of Wharton's MBA program, analyzed the return on investment of the MBA program with the precision of the financial techniques he learned during the program. He published his conclusions on his blog, titled mbacaveatemptor.[12] The result was that the net present value of the MBA investment over 10 years was negative...very negative. And as Josh Kaufman says in his book *The Personal*

MBA,[13] this is bad. It is the same as saying it is a ruinous investment. Schraga says, "Business school is a big risk. Should you choose to enroll, the only certainty is that you will shell out about $125,000. Such a figure correlates to a $1,500/month non-deductible loan repayment and a ten-year period of time in which you will not be able to save a red cent." According to his calculations (and always assuming that any increase in salary is pure and exclusively due to the program), you will need twelve years of "hard labor" just to pay back your tuition. That doesn't even take into consideration ROI, savings, or the quality of your life during that time…up to being forty. That is the very moment when your possibilities of continuing in the corporate life begin to fade away. Think about it twice. Better think about it three times.

In Europe, it is not much different. Tuition is lower there, but wages are also, and business schools set their prices depending on the applicants' expectations (not depending on the value the education really adds). I made the calculation for a European MBA, with a departing salary of € 53,000 (~ $69,000). NPV of an investment over ten years for a two-year MBA costing € 70,000 (~ $91,000) is negative considering a rate of return of 7 percent and bank interest of 4 percent if the applicant took a loan to cover the cost of the program.

If you want to calculate an estimate of the NPV of your MBA investment, you can find an NPV calculator at www.thembabubble.com/npv-calculator.

Any Investment in Education Is Good... Isn't It?

When I decided to apply to my MBA program, I did not do not even glimpse at all of these calculations. Do you want me to tell you how I decided that an MBA was a good investment?

When I knew I wanted to apply for the MBA program, I relied on a colleague who helped me prepare my admission. He had just completed his MBA degree from Harvard. I am deeply grateful to him for his generous attitude. Nevertheless, I did not do a suitable analysis of the advice he gave me. I made an enormous mistake.

He enjoyed his MBA experience very much and encouraged me to apply to the MBA program, too. His company paid his tuition and all of his and his family's expenses while he was enrolled in the program. When I told him I was worried about the cost, he said to me, "Do not worry. For the things that are worth it, there is always money." His words were enough for me....

But I followed the advice of someone who did not have to worry about the cost or ROI. What a huge mistake! I took only a few seconds to analyze the return on the most important investment I have ever made in my life. Unfortunately that is the way most people do it.

An article in the *Chicago Tribune* tells the story of another Harvard MBA graduate,[14] Joe Mihalic. He did not worry about the cost, either. Why would he worry if he had a ticket to a successful and prosperous career once being admitted to Harvard? The problem was that, unlike my colleague, nobody paid his loan off when he finished the program. More than ten years' worth of heavy debt awaited him, seriously limiting the way he could live the best years of his life. Mihalic assumed everything would take care of itself. "I was completely naïve," he said. If something went wrong with his job, it would be a financial disaster. "I felt trapped," he confessed. He was also limited in terms of risking anything at work or switching to a lower-paying job in which he could make more of a contribution to the world. His freedom was deeply affected. To get rid of debt as soon as possible, this brilliant professional decided to live like a Tibetan monk for some time: He sold his car, took roommates, and quit going to movies and restaurants.

This brilliant Harvard graduate was plagued by debt for years. Think about it the next time you see the advertising of one of the most prestigious European business schools:

"You do not need even one Euro to pursue our MBA degree."[15]

This school has an agreement with a bank. For anyone who is admitted to the program, the bank will grant a loan to finance it. In addition, fewer than 1 percent of those who get such loans fail to repay them. Why aren't more people rushing to apply?

Oh, sure, I see. After finishing the program, they will have to pay the loan. For years and years. But the fact that they can pay it back does not mean that it is a good investment. Price and value are not the same thing.

Business Plans Never Make It

If you are worrying about these numbers, you should also consider that things can go wrong. In fact, they usually do.

The disappointment among MBA graduates was already frequent ten years ago when I graduated. Since the 2008 financial crisis, things are getting even darker. Philip Delves Broughton tells in his book, *Ahead of the Curve*,[16] that many of his ex-colleagues from Harvard Business School working in financial services in 2006 lost their jobs amid the crisis. For those who stayed, bonuses diminished considerably. And they had a miserable quality of life. They worked infinite hours and, in many cases, took antidepressants or tranquillizers to be able to stand it day after day. In an article published in *The Economist*,[17] Broughton warns that to get an MBA is riskier than ever these days. And it is not only because of the financial crisis and the risk of getting a worse job when graduating but also because it is already obvious that an MBA is not even a requirement to be successful in business.

A January 2013 article in *The Wall Street Journal*[18] revealed the results of a study showing that salaries have decreased for the graduates of 62 percent of 186 business schools studied. This effect is also seen in top business schools, too. The article shows that for many graduates carrying heavy debt, nothing has changed, either in their wages or in their careers. Is the economic crisis the only cause? No, of course not. Companies' needs have changed, and so has their perception of the value added by business schools.

A *BusinessWeek* article[19] tells the story of a student who spent lots of money on an MBA. After fruitless efforts to get a job, she began to receive recommendations from her school to get an unpaid internship. "To hear that was like a nail in my heart," she said. She had to start over from the very bottom.

In Europe, things are even worse. The economic situation is really dark, and employment is deteriorating. Many MBA graduates have difficulty finding jobs.

Even ten years ago, I heard many of these discouraging stories. For example, one of my colleagues was a father who ran through all of his savings pursuing an MBA. Upon not getting a decent job offer, he requested an appointment with the president of the business school. He asked for an explanation for the gap between the information available in the school's rankings and the reality of the market. My colleague told me later that the explanation he received was, "We have to strain to look good in the rankings because applicants look at them to choose the school they want to attend."

I also had to go through an internship for one year, receiving only 500 € (~ $ 660) per month. And I was

Any Investment in Education Is Good... Isn't It?

not the only MBA graduate in that situation. Some of them stayed in that situation even longer than I did.

Why do you think that will not happen to you? Because of what they tell you in the informative meetings or in the leaflets?

They are selling you the program and the school. They want your money. It is OK that they do that. They do their work.

Nevertheless, when it is your turn to buy, do not forget to do your consumer's work. You should not believe that MBAs are healthy only because someone tells you they are cholesterol free.

5
MBAs Are Cholesterol Free

A half-truth is a whole lie.

Jewish Proverb

Some years ago, a recognized Spanish brand of olive oil presented an innovation in its marketing strategy. Its packaging was already attractive and well designed. But a change in a small detail made the sales explode. There was a new legend in its label that stood out. It said, "Cholesterol free." This oil was more expensive than the others, and consumers perceived it as being healthier.

Maybe you knew it already: *No vegetable oil has cholesterol*. Nevertheless, the strategy worked wonderfully. However, some time later, a few voices started questioning the ethics of this marketing message.

Today, the same oil brand still says it is cholesterol free, but it explains immediately that no vegetable oil has cholesterol.

Have they lied? No. Is it against the law? At first glance, it wasn't at the moment. Nevertheless, if many

The MBA Bubble

consumers made the mistake of believing it was the only olive oil in the market that was cholesterol free and they bought it because of that, the company might have been accused of deceitful marketing.

That is what deceitful marketing is—marketing that induces consumers to make mistakes. I want you to avoid making mistakes in buying your education.

After twelve years of working in marketing departments, I must admit that finding the balance between a responsible marketing message and one that creates results is not an easy task. It must be even more difficult for business schools because they do not have a consumers' association that forces them to practice what they communicate.

In any case, I am not going to affirm (for the moment) that business schools lie in their marketing messages. In fact, a few months ago, one of the most popular blogs in France published an article I wrote in French about the nonsense of getting an MBA.[20] It was the success of that article that made me decide to write this book. The author of the blog proposed to change the tittle to "They Lied to You: Why MBAs Are Not a Good Investment," but I did not agree with this tittle. The final title was "Do not Make a Mistake: Why MBAs Are Not a Good Investment." It is not that I think business schools are transparent and ethical in what they communicate, but that, in many aspects, it is not possible to accuse them of lying.

MBAs Are Cholesterol Free

The brilliant Seth Godin affirms in his book *All Marketers Are Liars*[21] that indeed everybody tells lies to themselves. We each have our own story in our head, and we tell ourselves it is true. The best marketing strategies are those that tell stories consumers want to hear.

I invite you to avoid lying to yourself and completing the missing information in the story someone else tells you with the information you want to hear. If business schools said to you that MBAs are cholesterol free, they would not be lying. But you should not believe that getting an MBA will have a positive impact in your health based on that information.

Do I want to say that marketing has ethical issues? Not necessarily. But in my opinion, when companies forget to add real value to their customers and to fulfill their promises (or at least make the story that customers told themselves come true), they will have problems.

In her book *J'ai fait HEC, et je m'en excuse*[22] (*I Went to HEC and I Am Sorry*), the French journalist Florence Noiville did a critical retrospective analysis on the education she received from her school, HEC. (It offers one of the most prestigious MBA programs in Europe.) She said that the most important doctrine she got from her school was the supreme goal of maximizing the bottom line by any means. She corroborated that concept throughout her career. Whenever she was asked to present financial results, those in charge would say to her, "Florence, how can we make more profit? The rest we don't care about." This culture of getting more profit by any means without caring about the consequences pushed her to make a career change to journalism and resign half of her salary.

Before that change, Noiville had been a marketing assistant at a tobacco company, where she participated in the design of a marketing campaign. The goal was to attract teenagers in an effort to gain "new consumers" and market share. The campaign included free samples of caps, glasses, and other products at ski sites and discotheques, which allowed the company to avoid the legal restrictions on other forms of publicity. The brand attempted to look "cool" to teenagers.

Noiville also tells the story of one of her colleagues from HEC, a publicist for a big publicity company. She took part in the design of a campaign focused on the health benefits of a food product, yet knowing it was not healthy at all.

None of these students ever learned to question their ethical responsibility for such actions at business school.

What makes you think that business schools are going to use different marketing techniques than those they teach? I will ask you again to use your good skepticism. *"How can we get more profit? The rest we don't care about."*

A Marketing Lesson

MBAs Are Cholesterol Free

Don't get me wrong. I have nothing against marketing or sales. On the contrary, since I decided to become independent, I am more than sensitive to the fact that sales and marketing are key. These functions are the survival guarantee for any prosperous company. I market, and I sell my products, and if you are reading this book, it is because you knew it thanks to the marketing I did to sell it to you. However, I consider myself to be a black sheep in the marketing world. I like to communicate only products and services in which I believe, and I was lucky to work (almost) always at leading companies that sold products that provided a real value to customers.

That's why I believe that ethical sales and marketing efforts create prosperous companies and benefit society. Unethical sales and marketing efforts lead to situations like this horrible financial crisis.

The most successful entrepreneurs and companies, which are, in fact, those that I admire the most, ask themselves this question first: "How can I add value to customers and to society?"

As soon as they have an answer, they ask this:

"How can I obtain a substantial benefit from this value?"

If they find a good answer for the second question, they put hands to work to create that value proposition,

55

communicating it to the world with the best marketing techniques.

These entrepreneurs and companies have changed the world. They have made life easier, and they have become rich. Good for them.

Other companies have lost sight of the importance of adding value to society and to their customers. Their main concern is only "How can we get more profit? The rest we don't care about." Unfortunately, the answer is not often "by adding more value" because that step normally increases expenses. Often the answer to this question is "increasing the perceived value of the product, regardless of how."

Let me clarify that I do not think there is anything wrong with increasing the perceived value of a product *if the value is real*. Why shouldn't a company charge more for a product if it contributes to a quality solution? But do you think that all companies are interested in adding real value to you?

Business schools' marketing suggests benefits of their programs that are not real.

Why do they do it? Because it works, of course. MBAs have been an excellent business for decades, and business schools do not have any incentive to change…until the market decides it is time for the bubble to burst. An article from a *Harvard Business Review* blog written by Professor Michael Ryall titled

"The MBA Tuition Bubble"[23] suggests that the business-school industry is aware of the little value added to students. However, they are very happy with the status quo as high tuition and a growing number of applicants finance useless research activity and the construction of new buildings.

Probably the first to denounce the corruption in business-schools' marketing was Henry Mintzberg through his book *Managers, Not MBAs*.[24] According to Mintzberg, the most prestigious schools are the worst. Their marketing materials might boast headlines like "Let the management faculty help you fly above the clouds for a global perspective of business." Or "The fast track for success just got faster." Or "[By finishing the program] you'll rank as one of the most highly qualified professionals in the world." Those are the stories you want to hear, but they are not reality. There is no fast track for success. To think that one buys a ticket to top management positions by reading a few business cases under pressure is an illusion. It is also unrealistic to believe that an MBA qualifies someone more for management. Mintzberg was affirming already in 2004 that this was a threat to society. Unfortunately, the origins of the 2008 financial crisis showed that he was right.

Business schools lead you to believe many myths through their marketing stories and the ones you tell yourself. I invite you to analyze many of them. Here is one example:

The MBA Bubble

"The MBA is indispensable to access to top management positions."

This one is good. You probably believe it. I believed it myself. What makes you think that the MBA is indispensable?

I am not going to deny that in management consulting or investment banking, an MBA is valued and is often a requirement to climb the corporate ladder.

But according to Josh Kaufman, author of *The Personal MBA*, only between 2.5 and 5 percent of the 200,000 MBA graduates worldwide each year are hired in these sectors.[25] Ouch! So if you have an MBA, you have at least a 95 percent chance of not ending up in one of those sectors. Some business schools (usually the most expensive) place a higher percentage of graduates in these sectors, but even graduates of those schools who are hired by these sectors are not the majority. There are also plenty of examples showing that even if it is often expected, an MBA is not *always* a requirement to work in these sectors. The author of an article posted at Gurusblog[26] who holds a top European MBA and has a management position in the financial sector affirms that an MBA was never a requirement for any of the positions he held and that he never hired anyone because they held the degree. Ouch again!

So let's see what happens to the rest of the 95 percent of the MBA graduates who do not go into management consulting or investment banking. Let me tell you about my experience. The MBA was never a requirement for any of the positions I held. Only one out of the seven bosses I had in my professional career (always in big leading companies) held an MBA degree, and he was not one of the most brilliant managers for whom I worked. No one ever asked me about my MBA in any job interview. Also, a few years ago, I took advantage of the services provided by an outplacement consulting service, which helped me find a job when I moved to France. My MBA degree did not factor into my being selected for the position.

Earlier, I mentioned Christian Schraga, the Wharton MBA who calculated the NPV of his education investment.[27] He also affirms that he never talks about his MBA and that his colleagues do not care about his pedigree. The most important thing to succeed, he says, is the way he plays the game.

In 2006, *BusinessWeek* led a study on the impact of the MBA in the careers of 500 of the highest-paid executives listed by Standard & Poor's. What's the conclusion? That the MBA is not a requirement to accede to top management positions.[28]

Again, be a skeptic in the good way. Try to find articles or interviews online featuring arguments that support the MBA's value. Maybe you will find some articles that affirm that an MBA is a requirement for top management positions or that it will put you on the fast track to success or that it makes a real difference in helping you face the financial crisis…. If you do find some, *I'll bet they were written by someone who has an interest in a business school* or was published in media in which business schools collaborate, such as forums and specialized MBA websites. It is most likely not objective information about the market, but it has been frequent enough information through the past decades.

Are the arguments in these articles lies? Essentially not because one can argue that it is someone's opinion. One can say that it is logical that someone who sells MBAs thinks they are valuable. But MBA applicants have read this kind of information again and again through the years, and they ended up believing that it is what the market requires. Well, *it is not*.

Many times, business schools publicize their programs through press releases. Just in case you don't know, let me explain to you how press releases work. Not everything you read in newspapers is the result of rigorous journalistic research. Sometimes journalists have a special interest in writing an article about a specific topic and in interviewing certain people. Many times, companies send press releases to the media to publicize information that is in their best interest. *For years, business schools have benefited from their reputation as university programs to access prestigious media. They opine about the labor market as if they were impartial. Well, they are not.* They say things that favor their business.

A CareerBuilder.com article titled "When Having an MBA Is Important"[29] is a blatant MBA marketing statement that conveys no impartial opinion from a labor-market expert, but rather from someone who wrote a book for MBA graduates affirming that an MBA can get you hired in a tough economy. I also read an article in a leading Argentine newspaper, *La Nacion*, titled "To Study Abroad: A Privilege for a Few?"[30] Harvard, Stanford, and some top European business schools tell their charming stories in it. The author affirms that an MBA is considered a sure investment because it guarantees a job as a manager in a big company. I wrote to the author to ask her how she corroborated the information. She never answered. Any expert in the labor market knows that it is an aberration to make such a claim. It seems more than evident to me that the article was motivated by a press release and that the author simply repeated the declarations of the representative of a business school.

I also read an article in the Spanish newspaper *CincoDías* titled "The Arrival of the Third-Generation MBAs."[31] The article was written by the representatives of various business schools. It looks like objective information clarifying that no degree guarantees a job in tough times, but the complete article contains eloquent phrases like "In some positions nowadays, it is not even conceived that a professional stagnates in his or her initial bachelor's education".

It is marketing disguised as objective and independent information, and it is repeated frequently.

Before I began my MBA, I became aware of marketing campaigns from my business school that said the degree would result in an immediate increase in salary. When these expected increases didn't happen, they said that one can expect a long-term return on investment. It made me think of the tobacco ads that invite smokers to use cigarettes to relax and to maximize the excitement of an adventure—two completely opposite benefits.

Here is another common business school marketing message:

> "*The MBA increases employability and opens doors to reinvent yourself.*"

Let me remind you how the job market works: Companies look for *specific experience* in a candidate first. This experience is meant to minimize the cost of training and reduce risk. If a company's recruiter does not find a candidate through internal promotion or networking, he or she will hire a human resources consultant to look for the ideal candidate who has the exact experience they need. About 80 percent of all job offers are never published.

I will not deny it. If two candidates have the exact same level of experience and/or equivalent recommendations, an MBA can be a differentiating factor. But a candidate who spent two years in the job market getting valuable and specific experience instead of going to business school will beat any candidate who spent two years and hundreds of thousands of dollars getting an MBA.

If you conduct a cost–benefit analysis of an MBA degree, you will see that it will compensate you much more to focus on getting good experience and networking in a growing sector than to get an MBA. Experience is the key to getting the best jobs. The degree is a nice decoration in your résumé.

I guess you think that indeed networking is one of the key benefits of the MBA, and I propose to analyse this and the myth of employability later on. In any case I assure you that those who do not have an MBA can be as effective in high quality network building.

As for the possibility of making a career change as the result of getting an MBA, there is no expectation as unrealistic as this one. Even the director of professional careers at my business school said to me that it is almost impossible to make a career change without previous experience in the function or the sector. Of course he said that after I had "bought" the MBA.

If you believe that an MBA will help you make a career change, where did you get this idea from? Did you read it in a leaflet? Or hear it in the media? Was it the statement of someone involved in the business of promoting a business school?

Philip Delves Broughton describes in his book *Ahead of the Curve*[32] how this turns out to be a false promise: "If you don't have experience in an industry, they don't want you." And we are talking about one of the most prestigious business brands: Harvard. Obviously, things are not going to be better in other business schools. If you want a career change, you will have to fight a lot. Job offers for MBA graduates need two to four years of professional experience in an industry and/or job function. Christian Schraga also affirms that the notion that an MBA offers the opportunity for a career change is a "half truth" from business schools.

Maybe you think that it is valuable to associate yourself with a prestigious business brand. Well, if you believe this, maybe you are a ranking addict. Rankings are the most effective and least transparent marketing tool of business schools. They are irresistible bait for hungry and naïve professionals.

6
The Rankings: Bait for the Naïve

There are three kinds of lies: lies, damned lies, and statistics.

Mark Twain

I am going to assume that you have researched what rankings really mean. If you did not, it is quite possible that you let yourself be impressed by the grandiloquence of what it means to be (or not to be) in a top-ranked business school.

Too many people believe that the pedigree associated with a top-ranked business school is going to give them power they cannot get by themselves. If you are naïve and insecure, as many professionals in their twenties are, I am afraid that you will be easy prey for this strategic marketing weapon.

Before analyzing rankings in detail, I invite you to discover their importance in the marketing strategy of business schools.

The Most Effective Bait

The MBA Bubble

Life is hard. But you don't need me to tell you that. And it is hard to make decisions, especially those that bear a high cost if you get it wrong. Trust helps us make decisions.

Trust saves time and reduces uncertainty, making life easier. Brands strain to generate consumer confidence in their product or service as a trust-based marketing strategy. It is for that reason that innumerable certifications exist to try to impart confidence—for example, the ISO certification for quality standards.

As soon as trust is created, more than half of the marketing battle is won; that's why it is so important in a brand's marketing strategy.

When I had to decide where I was going to get my MBA, I consulted one of my colleagues, who holds an MBA from Harvard. As I trusted the Harvard brand, his advice was a confidence builder that accelerated my decision.

Business school rankings are one of the most effective confidence builders that influence a student's decision about the business school he or she will select. They were born as a need of the economic media to increase readers. Schools increased also their competitiveness to be among the top positions, and with that, rankings began to attract more and more attention.

I have to admit that rankings can convince even the most reticent:

The Rankings: Bait for the Naïve

- They are supported by prestigious publications, which tie their own brand image to the information (*Financial Times, BusinessWeek, The Economist, The Wall Street Journal, Forbes*, etc.).

- They facilitate in a simple and accessible way the most appreciated information: MBA graduates' average wages.

- They compare all business schools with an apparent transparence and objectivity through the same criteria.

But don't forget the old-business mantra "How can we make more profits? The rest we don't care about." One way business schools can make more profits is to achieve a top ranking because it is the main confidence builder that influences trust and decision making.

And how can business schools become better ranked? They could add more value to students and employers. But a more effective and *faster way to do it is to lie and manipulate the information*. It seems obvious to me that the information published is not exact. John Byrne, the father of business school rankings at *BusinessWeek*, says, "The schools lie. Much like some students, the schools play games to get better grades."[33] I do not doubt it.

You may be wondering how it is possible to manipulate the rankings. Don't publications audit the information they receive from business schools? Isn't their reputation at stake?

Well, they don't audit the information. They probably do not have the resources to do it. And there is no transparency with regard to the veracity of the results. An article in the Spanish newspaper *El País*[34] states that only the *Financial Times* audits the information from barely 30 percent of the schools through independent consultants. But taking into account the lessons the society learned in the financial crisis of 2008, I do not trust blindly in the results of the audits. If the schools do lobby with the publications, what is the guarantee that the information is accurate?

Juan Manuel Roca is a Spanish PhD and business journalist. He wrote a book in 2009 that revealed his analysis of the business school industry and its responsibility in the 2008 crisis, with the support of the dean of Thunderbird. The book is titled *MBAs, ¿Angeles o Demonions?* (*MBAs, Angels or Demons?*). He affirms in his book that business schools complain about the way their competitors try to "influence" publications to get a better position in the rankings. Some prestigious business schools even question the veracity of the information on wages supplied by other schools, adducing that nobody controls it and that this information is very easy to manipulate. "It is a fact that nobody can verify what this former student is earning," declares a professor from a prestigious business school. Believe me, I was there, and I don't buy it, either. In 2007, *The Wall Street Journal* put its ranking of business schools under review after admitting that

The Rankings: Bait for the Naïve

several schools had "played" with the information.[35] Do you still have faith in what the rankings say?

You Will Believe What You Want to Believe

Even if you think business schools would never practice "financial academic engineering" with the rankings, (an expression used by Juan Manuel Roca[36] comparing the manipulation of rankings with the financial manipulations done by Enron), much of the apparently objective information available in rankings is flooded with considerable subjectivity.

I will explain it to you in a simple way.

First, let's address the most common apparently objective fact: An MBA graduate's wages will increase.

Christian Schraga, the Wharton graduate,[37] says it in a very direct way: This is one of the "half truths" of business schools (I would like to call it a half lie). *Not all MBA graduates answer the surveys that build the rankings.* In general, those who earn lower wages are unwilling to answer because they don't feel proud about it. Human beings are like that. Schraga did not answer the survey. In my case, I could not find the e-mail that contained the questionnaire. I do not mean that I have doubts that it was sent; I might have erased it. But even if I could have found it, I would not have answered, either, for the same reasons. According to the *Financial Times*, only 48 percent of the surveys were answered in the last edition.[38] Assuming that most of the

69

The MBA Bubble

unanswered surveys belong to the lowest-salary graduates, this fact pulls up the average numbers in a considerable way.

In addition to this, there is another factor, which though not subjective, compromises objectivity in the interpretation of average wages. If Bill Gates earns one billion dollars a year and I earn zero, the statistics say that we earn $500 million each. Statistics are like that. The fact is that the percentage of the MBA graduates who find jobs at investment banks or management consulting firms raise the average wages because their awful jobs with ninety-hour work weeks are well paid, especially regarding bonuses. Well, it is logical that if they work twice as much, they will earn twice as much. A *BusinessWeek* article suggestively titled "The Devil Is in The Details"[39] shows that the wages of MBA graduates from prestigious business schools range widely. So you can work ninety-hour work weeks in the consulting sector and earn $250,000 a year or be employed in the media sector and earn $20,000 a year, even though you hold a Wharton MBA.

Not everyone pays attention to this detail, but in many rankings, wages are adjusted to the purchasing-power parity of the different countries in which graduates are employed. For example, if a school has many graduates being employed in developing countries, wages are not "realistic." I wish the cost of attending business school were adjusted to the purchasing-power parity of the applicant's country of origin, but it is not.

The Rankings: Bait for the Naïve

Finally, do not forget that if you come to the conclusion that you will earn the wage you see in rankings by getting your MBA, you are going to get a really bad grade in logic. You would be coming to a "correlation = causality" conclusion without having demonstrated causality. Many other factors can account for MBA graduates having high wages. For example, they work longer-than-average hours, so an average hourly income multiplied by the number of hours worked looks like a high wage. If you start working sixteen hours a day from now on, your salary probably will increase more than it would if you were to complete an MBA. Another cause of high salaries could be the pre-selection of business schools—they admit only talented candidates, and talented people usually earn more.

Now let's consider a second apparently objective fact revealed by rankings: MBA graduates experience career evolution and earn employer recommendations.

It is clear that if MBA graduates invest such a large amount of money and such a great effort in the pedigree, it is because they believe they will get something valuable in return. Therefore, it is in their best interest to give a high grade to the school. Graduates complain when their schools lose positions in the rankings.[40] On the other hand, graduates cannot compare the various schools objectively; neither can employers because they do not know enough about all the schools or enough graduates from various schools. What sense does it make to include this information in the rankings? Its objectivity is non-existent.

71

The Filling That Fills Less

If we take as an example one of the most prestigious MBA rankings, the one published by the *Financial Times*, only 40 percent of the positions in the ranking are determined by salary variables. Another 12 percent are determined by graduates' recommendations and other factors that might have a (debatable) impact on one's career. Another 48 percent is composed of variables that could hardly demonstrate an impact on professional results: percentage of women (students and teachers), percentage of professors who hold a PhD, academic research, international experience, languages.... Half of the ranking is composed of factors that are politically correct and that increase the prestige of the school. But they do not add direct value to the student. In fact, the study of the AMLE[41] also comes to the conclusion that academic research done by the business schools and their PhDs has a modest impact on the practices of management compared to the research led by other sources such as consultants, journalists, or other professionals.

I invite you to consider how your career is going to improve if your school practices "financial academic engineering" to be better ranked and hires plenty of foreign female PhD professors and pushes them to publish a lot of articles. This happens. I've heard professors complain about the nonsense of the pressure that their schools place on them to publish.

Another important thing to keep in mind is that rankings are a picture of a moment in the professional career of the graduates a few years after graduation. They do not reflect long-term career satisfaction. In general, it reflects the golden moment of any professional career, with or without an MBA.

Trapped in Their Own Nets

Juan Manuel Roca affirms in his book[42] that many deans of prestigious schools criticize the strategy of focusing on rankings. The reality is, though, that they cannot live without them. Business schools are a great business, and rankings are an effective sales tool. A few years ago, Harvard and Wharton, two of the most prestigious business schools in the world, wanted to end this circus. They unilaterally stopped supplying information for the rankings because they thought they could thrive on the strength of their brands without exposing themselves to the tricks of pretentious schools trying to match their status. But this did not last very long. A few years later, they reversed their strategy. They could not give up fighting in the field where their rivals won more battles.

Another reason why rankings are such an effective "weapon" is that the higher a school gets in the rankings, the bigger its capacity becomes to attract the most brilliant professionals...and the capacity to take the credit for their success. This is a self-fulfilling prophecy, as suggested by the "Official MBA Guide."[43] Thanks to rankings, business schools guarantee their success in attracting and admitting only the most brilliant candidates. It seems logical that some schools get agreements with banks to give loans to students who are admitted. Banks know that even if the students don't graduate, they will still be able to pay the loans back.

The naïves, those who do not know how to evaluate their decision, those who feel insecure about themselves, those who do not know how to evaluate the labor market and the impact of pursuing an MBA, those who need a confidence builder—all of them are candidates for biting the fish hook. And the rankings are the most effective bait. I took the bait.

I believe the first confidence builder you must analyze before applying to an MBA program is *your self-confidence*. As professor Pfeffer from Stanford says, "If you are good enough as to be admitted, you have the talent to succeed, regardless." There is no position in the ranking of any business school that is more profitable than your self-confidence. If you need to develop new abilities, you can acquire them as you need them. If you are smart, you will be able to demonstrate it in an interview. If you work hard, you have a high probability that your effort will be recognized. Do not invest decades of your effort to pay your tuition while business schools take the credit. Thousands of professionals are successful without the MBA. What makes you think it is a condition for success?

It is not only your money you can lose by getting an MBA.

7
Selling One's Soul to the Devil

The most dangerous risk of all—the risk of spending your life not doing what you want on the bet you can buy yourself the freedom to do it later.

Randy Komisar, The Monk and the Riddle

*...wasting my money and my life,
I slowly began to give up....*

Excerpt of a song by the Spanish
singer and songwriter Joaquín Sabina

What would you do if a thief aimed at you with a gun and asked you to choose between your money and your life? I guess you would give him your money. Life is a human being's most important asset, although unfortunately most people become aware of this only when faced with a life-or-death situation. You could waste both your money and your life by getting an MBA.

If these words make you feel uncomfortable, let me warn you that this chapter is about my own values. I know that they are not values shared by all. I do not expect you to share them. Nevertheless, I recommend that you not skip this chapter because it is probable that you simply have not stopped to think about many things.

The generation to which I belong and to which you probably belong, too, has absorbed the worst of the Industrial Age and the transition into the new millennium. My generation has benefited from the democratization of comfort and technology. But the world's pace of change has increased exponentially to the point of making our lives increasingly frantic and the future increasingly unpredictable. Nevertheless, we continue operating with the paradigms of the Industrial Age.

You probably grew up perceiving that a college degree was a ticket to a prosperous and sure future, as your parents taught you. You also may have grown up valuing the effort as a guarantee of success because it is what has allowed previous generations to overcome wars and crises. But you have had tools that have allowed you to achieve tasks infinitely faster than previous generations. Also, you have been bombarded by infinite marketing messages that try to persuade you that you need something more in your life to be happy.

The result of all of that is that millions of people live alienated in unsatisfactory lives, lacking purpose, running faster to earn more money to spend it trying to anesthetize dissatisfaction and emptiness. They buy things they do not need with the money they do not have to impress people they cannot stand. They dream of the day they will retire to finally enjoy life. Many people try to run faster in this ridiculous circle to accumulate as much money as possible to end the torture as soon as they can.

This is a sad reality, and an MBA degree makes it even sadder because it accentuates this vicious circle of unhappiness. The worst thing is that this reality is not perceived as a problem in the first years of professional life, and it is very easy to be trapped by it. But soon, personal and emotional accounts fall into red numbers.

The MBA Trap

Within a few months after beginning my MBA, I realized that what I was learning there would not give me any competitive advantage in the short term for a simple reason: I was being taught to make top management decisions for an industrial company. And when I got out, I would have only the experience that would be applicable to a product manager's job, just like the one I had before I started the program.

Also, I would not be able to use that knowledge immediately. As Henry Mintzberg says in his book,[44] the risk for companies is that MBA graduates think they are qualified to make top management decisions just because they have discussed a few cases in class. Confidence without competence is arrogance. It was obvious to me. The AMLE study[45] shows that the MBA curriculum has only a minimal relationship with the factors that are essential for success in business.

The MBA Bubble

It made me wonder why companies would value an MBA graduate when (1) it is highly probable that he or she is a pretentious candidate trying to gain a positive return on his or her investment through higher wages and (2) his or her correlation with a higher added value is not clear. What is the benefit of hiring an MBA when a company can train a 22-year-old professional for much less than the salary demanded by an MBA and get the same results?

Again, business schools pre-select the most talented candidates. The MBA degree is like a "quality certification," but it does not add anything that the candidate did not have already.

But companies value one thing in MBA graduates, and I never thought about it when I applied for the MBA program. *Business schools train their students to become servants*, and big corporations really value that.

During an MBA program, the pace of study and the stress students experience is tremendous. Without exaggerating, a responsible full-time student studies between fourteen and sixteen hours per day for a minimum of six days per week. (And when I say "responsible student," I imply that there are also "tourist students" who take a year off, party often, learn how to cheat, and take advantage of their colleagues' hard work). Part-time students must add their study work load to their professional responsibilities and end up working and studying the same number of hours per day. Some schools grade students according to the Gauss curve, failing the 10 percent of students with the

Selling One's Soul to the Devil

lowest grades in each subject. That adds an additional pressure: the threat of being expelled from the school and losing tuition.

What emerges from MBA programs is the ideal "chopped meat" to manufacture the "burgers" for big corporations: talented and deep-in-debt professionals, who are trained to support the unbearable and to absorb unlimited amounts of information.

The problem with chopped meat is that, although it is very profitable for the one who chops it and for the one who eats the burger, the cow earns nothing in the process. Do you follow me?

Philip Delves Broughton makes this point repeatedly throughout his book.[46] He contends that business schools do not try to teach you to do everything; they force you to choose with their exceeding demands. For some students, this is not a problem. They are already accustomed to working between 80 and 100 hours per week at their previous jobs. They do not expect that to improve after finishing the MBA program. If that is not your case, it is possible that you bought yourself a nightmare. The jobs that correspond with the expected MBA wages demand infinite work hours. And when I say infinite, I mean that your life will literally belong to the company that hires you. According to Broughton, a Harvard student worked seventy-seven days nonstop during his summer internship at Goldman Sachs. Basically, he went to the office one day and never left. A Harvard MBA graduate employed at Morgan Stanley went to talk to students at the school. He told them that one week he spent 127 hours in the office. I will save you the calculation. One week contains a total of 168 hours. During his visit, he confessed that there were weeks and weeks in which he had barely seen the traits of his children in shadows below the sheets. Broughton affirms that this is the reality of most MBA graduates: ninety-hour work weeks. He confesses that many times he has asked himself a question that I also asked myself more than once: *What am I doing?* Many of the Harvard MBA graduates who talked to students about their professional successes showed the failure and unhappiness in their personal lives. Business school had forced them to choose, and they had made their choice.

MBA graduates' wages can be higher than non MBAs', but their hourly salary is frequently lower than that of the cleaning assistant. What sense does it make to work 100 percent more to earn 50 percent more than the average? If this completely unbalanced life attracts you and you want to earn more money, wouldn't it be more logical to save the MBA money and devote yourself to creating an alternative business after work?

The truth is that even if hard work does not scare you right now and you find it stimulating, not many people can stand the pace without a "little help." In the documentary titled *Inside Job* about the financial crisis of 2008,[47] you can see the kind of lifestyle led by professionals on Wall Street. Drugs and prostitution are the common currency. I am not at all surprised.

If you want to get an MBA to learn how to work eighty hours a week to increase your income because you

Selling One's Soul to the Devil

believe that it is not anything that you can learn on your own...well, I believe that you are ruining your life and that you can learn how to work as a slave without needing to spend a fortune in tuition.

Please think about it. You have only one life. If you are under thirty right now, you may not have perspective about how your life is going to be, but there will be a point at which you will be keenly aware of everything you missed in your life. If you take the wrong train, it will be very difficult—even impossible to change your destination later. Although now it could seem like an easy thing to do in the future and that you will always have the option to change your path, the reality is that you will have to really fight if you want to change.

Maria Jesus Álava Reyes says in her book *Trabajar sin Sufrir* (*Work Without Suffering*)[48], "The feeling that the best years of your life have been stolen is devastating [....] There are millions of people who experience the tragedy of not being the masters of their lives." She tells the story of someone who might be a typical MBA graduate: A thirty-eight-year-old consultant with endless schedules, infinite trips, his marriage in crisis, and a three-year-old child whom he could rarely see. He was medicated for anxiety for one year. He had dedicated thirteen years of his life to his company. He was expecting to be able to negotiate fewer responsibilities so that he could spend at least the weekends with his family. But it was an illusion. To be able to have control of his life was an illusion.

The MBA Bubble

Broughton affirms that many of his Harvard colleagues had a number in their minds. When they reached it, they would leave everything. A chapter of his book is titled "The Factory of Unhappy People." His colleagues were accepting jobs that would make them miserable with the hope of absorbing the pain long enough for success to make them happy. And then everything would have been worth it.[49] I think it is a sad illusion.

Florence Noiville, the author of the book *J'ai fait HEC et je m'en excuse*[50] (*I Went to HEC and I'm Sorry*), tells how she passed from being the black sheep of her class as she sank the wage statistics when she became a journalist to being envied by her colleagues for her personal and professional fulfilment at age forty. Many of them struggle to give sense to their lives. Some of them come to the point of "living a secret life." During the day, they are employed at the bank; by night, they are Arab translators or psychotherapists. They take on additional jobs in secret so that they will not lose their credibility.

The most ridiculous thing of all is that most of these professionals who have run faster all those years arrive at the age of forty having had a less satisfactory life and often having generated fewer assets that those who went slower, enjoyed life, and spent less on expensive toys (including the MBA).

Many ambitious young people think about their professional future as if it were a question of accumulating power and money as quickly as possible. Not only the expectation of obtaining this through an

MBA is an illusion; also, they do not realize that the best years of their lives will have faded away very quickly.

Nobody regrets having spent less time in the office when the last days of life arrive. To spend seventy or eighty hours per week in a depressing job you can lose overnight makes no sense in the bigger picture. Do not wait until it is too late to see it.

The Misunderstood Hard-Work Culture

One of the mental models that pushed me to make a mistake regarding my decision to get an MBA is this one: "If you work hard, you will succeed, as your effort is the guarantee of your success."

I know that to question this mental model is delicate. It is a mental model that is shared by many people whom I admire. In any case, I will admit they are right on one point: If someone wants to be successful without making any effort, it will be really hard. But the problem with this mental model is that *it focuses on the effort itself and not on the value added by the effort*. It is indeed the value what matters, and the effort and hard work can be a requirement to get this value…or not.

What happens many times is that people choose the most difficult path only because their work-hard ethic makes them value it more than they value a more efficient way to reach their destination. It happened to me with my MBA: The financial and personal effort

The MBA Bubble

was huge, and my mental model made me think that the reward was proportional to the effort. But it was not; I only chose the most difficult way.

Most of the things that are worthwhile in life require hard work, but hard work itself is not a guarantee at all. In fact, humanity and the economy progressed thanks to the discovery of more efficient ways to do things. Under this point of view, the MBA is not a synonym of progress but the opposite.

You will probably argue that, like it or not, today's world is more demanding and competitive and that you need to train yourself to face to the growing demands of the job market. You will have to excuse me, but I do not think that being trained to work like a dog until you are exhausted will help you win the battle beyond the heart attack you will have at age forty-five.

Recently, I was watching a documentary on French television on new trends in education. They were telling the story of a couple living in Hong Kong. They decided to educate their twins to face the requirements of the twenty-first century because they had come to the conclusion that competition for jobs will be much harder in the future. They thought that winning the game against thousands of other well-prepared candidates will be increasingly complex. As a result, they were forcing their eight-year-old children to get up at 5 a.m., to train for an hour in the swimming pool and compete with older children, then return to the house to do their math homework. By the time they went to school, they had already had three more hours of activities and preparation that the rest of children. However, when the teacher asked them to give their opinion about a topic in class, the exercise became almost impossible for them, and they would turn in their assignments much later than their classmates. These children were being educated to be the best slaves of an increasingly demanding master, not to be free, creative, masters of their lives. One of them told a journalist that he "knew" that everything he wanted in his life would require hard work. It means that if something gives him some pleasure and turns out to be easy for him because it comes from one of his talents, he will probably reject it. That is the myth of the hard-work culture for me—that it is wise to choose the most difficult path for the exaltation of effort itself. These children, in spite of their parents' intentions, will probably lose the game against those who could come up with creative solutions naturally. This is not the reality that I want for my son.

Instead of training of future generations to win in a competitive game that will make them unhappy, I believe we should teach them to create their own game... and to win it. I invite you to listen to Sir Ken Robinson's talks at TED[51]. They are very inspiring. Future generations need more freedom, abundance, happiness, and respect for their resources and the environment, don't you think? I am not talking about teaching them to be poor and happy; I am talking about redefining wealth.

Another Life Is Possible

The MBA Bubble

Some will argue that even if it is good to have a purpose in life, the undeniable reality is that you need money to live a serene life. And to earn money, you need to make sacrifices.

Well, I do not value poverty, and I think that the first thing someone can do for the poor is to not be one of them. But to me, owning a few fancy suits and a nice car when you die is not a worthy prize for having lived.

Some time ago, I began to look for evidence that it is possible to live otherwise. That's why I started to meet entrepreneurs who are masters of their lives, and I learned a lot from them. They live in freedom and finance their life experiences in a smart way. They live life with purpose, enjoy every moment, and build their reality with effort but without sacrifice. Many of them earn a lot of money, and some of them do so at the age at which I was going into debt with my MBA degree. Their way is not easy, but they did choose the best way, not the most difficult. They are not slaves of the system. They are not anonymous cogs in machinery that consumes lives.

If you think entrepreneurship is not the path for you, let me tell you that I also know many people who are masters of their lives being employees. They choose companies with a mentality of results and not of servitude. These people are professional and responsible, and once they have done their work, they live their lives. In general, they are financially responsible and are not devoted to consumerism. They are not in debt. Many of them reach the age of forty-

Selling One's Soul to the Devil

five with more assets than many ambitious, older executives who were pushed to buy themselves an image for their careers. Some of them, simply by having been constant, earn more today than some MBAs. And they have a higher quality of life, which represents immeasurable wealth.

Maybe you think that finding companies that offer flexible conditions is almost impossible, especially in the tough times we are living in now. But I assure you that these companies exist. If you consider it to be impossible, it will be. You create your life first in your mind, and the impossible is only impossible in your mind. Today there are companies like Evernote that do not impose timetables on employees, and many more allow employees to work from home. I have a friend who works for an office in Madrid but lives between Berlin and Mallorca Island, and he works from home. Today, many companies value creativity, responsibility, top performance and talent over servility.

Before finishing this chapter, I invite you to ask yourself a few questions. I wish I had asked myself these questions before I pursued my MBA degree:

- Imagine for a moment that you are on your deathbed. What kind of life would you like to have lived that would allow you to leave in peace, without regrets?

- What makes you happy?

- What would you do with your life if you had the complete certainty that you cannot fail?

You are the master of these answers—unless you never ask the questions. Live your own life, not the one that others say you have to live.

I stop here with the thoughts and values in mind that pushed me out of the corporate world to embrace uncertainty. I do not expect you to share them—just think about them.

Do you still think that making money is more important than being happy? I agree that money is very important. But pursuing an MBA is far from being the best strategy for becoming rich.

8
If You Want to Be Rich, Don't Get an MBA

I'd like to live as a poor man with lots of money.

Pablo Picasso

If the whole idea of enjoying life looks a bit unrealistic to you and your dream is to get rich first and then buy the life you want, this chapter is for you. And if you want to be happy but with a very healthy bank account, this chapter is for you, too.

The first thing I am going to say about wealth is that many authors who write about prosperity and wealth make it clear: *A job will not make you rich.*

If you want to be wealthy, at some moment of your life, you will have to create a source of income other than your salary. This is an evident and crushing reality: If you sell your time to others, you will quickly reach a limit in your capacity to generate income.

In his book *Rich Dad, Poor Dad*,[52] Robert Kiyosaki said that the rich do not work for money; they generate assets that work for them. If you want to learn how to work for money, go to school. If you want to learn how to work even harder, you should get an MBA.

Ok, some top managers earn millions (and they are therefore millionaires). Some people still think they can get to those positions with an MBA, as if the *BusinessWeek* study was not convincing enough.[53] Do you want some more proof that an MBA will not get you there? If you look at the degrees of CEOs of the CAC 40 (the main stock exchange index in France), you will see that the MBA is nothing but an "optional" degree.[54] In some companies, it is still desirable to climb the corporate ladder. These companies represent a very low percentage of the companies in the market, and you do not need an MBA if your biggest ambition in life is to climb to a top management position.

But let's go back to the topic that interests you: how to be rich. "Show me the money." *If you want to be rich, you must be entrepreneur, investor, or both.* By a simple matter of statistics, your probability of becoming a rock star, sports star, or Standard & Poor's CEO are very low (and believe me, the MBA will not increase your probability of becoming a Standard & Poor's CEO).

The richest men in the world are entrepreneurs and do not have MBAs. Many of them have no degree at all or have quitted college when they realized that it was only teaching them to be employees and to obey. Today these people hire the ones who have degrees. Consider the cases of Mark Zuckerberg with Facebook, Bill Gates with Microsoft, Steve Jobs with Apple, Amancio

If You Want to Be Rich, Don't Get an MBA

Ortega with Zara–Inditex, Richard Branson with Virgin, or Ingvar Kamprad with Ikea. And there are a lot of anonymous rich men and women who have never sat in a college classroom to learn how to be corporate slaves.

To become an entrepreneur, you need some business sense, and many young professionals come to the fatal conclusion that the MBA will provide the training they need. After all, the leaflets from business schools talk about entrepreneurship, don't they?

I could tell you many true stories about MBA graduates who put their entrepreneurial dreams aside. I do not have statistical studies that demonstrate this reality, but I have an MBA, and I know what happens when going to business school. In an article on his blog at *El Mundo* newspaper, investor Alejandro Suárez Sanchez Ocaña tells the case of an MBA student who said he would create a business when he found a lucrative idea.[55] Suárez adduces that this student was deceiving himself and that he was not an entrepreneur because he expected to find a brilliant idea. I believe that what was happening to that student is that he did not have a dime left after paying his tuition. This student realized that he needed to give intensive care to his personal finances before being able to consider entrepreneurship. Even if tuition is financed by family contributions, entrepreneurship after the program tends to be impossible because one's funds are typically not unlimited, and personal expenses need to be financed, too. But business schools sell the illusion that money will always be available for a good idea.

The MBA Bubble

Philip Delves Broughton describes aptly in his book[56] what happens in business school regarding the desire to be an entrepreneur: It fades away, even for those who already are entrepreneurs. To start with, business schools' "entrepreneurship" professors usually are not entrepreneurs themselves. A Broughton's classmate described the classes to be "like hearing virgins talking about sex." Professors' disinterest regarding students' projects is evident: Broughton noted that his professor invested only seven minutes to his project, a fact that made him feel completely demoralized. The idea of becoming an entrepreneur never left him, but after graduating, he realized that the payments on his $175,000 student loan would become due shortly. The pressure to earn an income and therefore to get a job became unbearable. In spite of having made a solid business plan for a business with good potential, Broughton realized that he needed cash to finance his family's expenses. Finally he abandoned his project and decided to offer freelance consulting.

But there is a factor that is more compelling than personal finances that keeps most students from becoming entrepreneurs after graduating: *culture*. An entrepreneur is a visionary who tries to break away from the crowd and create his or her own rules. The MBA program, on the contrary, attracts people who want to be in the middle of the crowd. For that reason, most entrepreneurs ignore MBA programs.[57] The consequence is that those who graduate from one of these programs eternize in the middle class, employed as white-neck servants on others' projects.

If You Want to Be Rich, Don't Get an MBA

According to reports from business schools as prestigious as Harvard or the Spanish IESE, only 4 percent of their graduates become entrepreneurs. As Mintzberg says, the faculty of "entrepreneurship" has become fashionable in recent years for business schools, but their real goal is to lead graduates into the corporate world of big, established business. It is not surprising that only a small percentage of successful entrepreneurs have an MBA. "I should have utilized that time to set up more business. True entrepreneurs get out of school as fast as they can and get on with life," asserted one successful American entrepreneur.[58]

In fact, as Juanma Roca suggests,[59] the "entrepreneurship" faculty arises in many business schools due to their inability to find students jobs at the level of their promises. Do you remember the MBA graduate from the *BusinessWeek* article who could not find a job and was advised to find an internship?[60] Guess what she did after realizing that the job thing was not working—she launched her own start-up. Do you still believe an MBA program is the best place to turn yourself into an entrepreneur?

Educating Yourself to Be an Entrepreneur and to Be Free

I am not affirming that you can be a millionaire without training. What I suggest is that it's not the diploma that will make you wealthier but the specialized knowledge applied to the resolution of a specific problem. Look what Napoleon Hill says in his book *Think and Grow Rich*:[61] "Knowledge will not attract money unless it is organized and intelligently directed through practical plans of action for the accumulation of money."

But that is not the goal of MBA programs, which focus on the accumulation of degrees. And debt. And a senseless pedigree.

To be fair, I will tell you what I did learn in business school: *A business is not a job, but a machine.* For the machine to work and move faster, all of the pieces must be calibrated and coordinated perfectly. If only one of them fails, the entire machine will stop working. Marketing, operations, finance, human resources, information systems, strategy...everything must be calibrated. You should have at least a notion of how these functions influence each piece of the machine in your business.

That's the only useful thing I learned. The technical knowledge I learned in each of those subjects was oriented to an industrial company from the previous century. The training I received in my MBA program is practically obsolete.

Today I can build a "Lean" start-up that subcontracts all services. For the company to thrive, I must employ techniques of twenty-first century marketing. Most of them are free and I can learn them in the courses that brilliant entrepreneurs teach for much less than a business school's tuition. Finance and accounting can be handled by an independent advisor for a reasonable monthly fee. I can subcontract operations duties and learn how to implement strategy in today's unpredictable business environment by reading a few books.

Josh Kaufman, author of *The Personal MBA*,[62] is sure that getting an MBA is a waste of time and money. Everything you need to learn about business can be learned reading the best ninety-nine business books available, which are most likely more up-to-date than the typical MBA program. You can see the list of these books on his website.[63] In fact his book summarizes the most important business concepts, which can give you the vision that you need for launching your own start-up.

Michael Ellsberg, author of *The Education of Millionaires*[64], reveals all the success skills that many wealthy people (most of them without diplomas) have developed to succeed. Ellsberg shows in his book that practical intelligence almost always beats academic intelligence, and dedicates a complete chapter of his book to the higher education bubble.

If I wanted to be trained as an entrepreneur with a global vision of a business, I would follow the training of real entrepreneurs who have succeeded the way I want —not academic professors. Many successful entrepreneurs teach their formula for success, and they have been helping others succeed in the same way. You can take advantage of their amazing coaching, their mentoring, a satisfaction guarantee, and a savings of about $100,000.

Learning Finance to Get Rich

But what if your strategy to achieve wealth is by investing instead of entrepreneurship? I wish I had better news—an MBA program is not the best place to learn how to invest, either. If you read any personal finance book, you will know that the best thing you can do to be wealthy is to get rid of debt as soon as possible and start investing early in your life. Why would you get more debt to get a degree? First, it will take you many years to pay back the tuition. Second, the finance they will teach you in the MBA program is not going to serve you but rather the companies for which you will work. And third, to be able to invest in an intelligent way, you need to have time to analyze your investments. How are you going to do that if you are working ninety hours a week?

Before spending a dime on a degree, buy a book on personal finance and wealth and/or take seminars with experts. If you do not do it as soon as possible, you will continue making mistakes that will damage your financial freedom. I made many, and the MBA was one of the biggest.

The expression "rat race" is probably familiar to you. It refers to useless effort. It is frequently used to describe the vicious circle of the middle class, with people running faster and faster on the corporate "wheel" that is compared to those in rat cages—both wheels keep the subject in the same place. Getting an MBA can perpetuate your futile effort in the rat race. Even if you have someone who finances this experience, you will not escape from the typical consumption dynamics of this ridiculous race.

In presenting a caricature of the middle-class mentality and the rat race, Robert Kiyosaki describes his "poor dad" as an educated man with many degrees whose highest aspiration was to work in better-paid jobs and receive better social benefits. When his "poor dad" needed money, he worked harder to earn it. Then, if he finally got the raise he wanted, he increased his expenses proportionally or went into debt. Banks and the government took the result of his supplementary efforts as interest and taxes. On the other hand, his "rich dad," a man without degrees who taught him everything he knew about business, was wondering instead how he could generate assets that worked for him, and he worked for others only if he needed to learn something.[65]

Getting an MBA can perpetuate your futile effort in the rat race. Even if you have someone who finances this experience, you will not escape from the typical consumption dynamics of this ridiculous race.

To keep your status in your corporate life and to build the image that will push you up the corporate ladder, your home, car, vacation spots, clothes, appearance, and kids' schools will have to match the image that is expected of a successful person.

If you do not enter this competition of appearances because you decide to save your money to create your

The MBA Bubble

own assets in the future, your image will begin to be one of someone who is projecting his or her future outside and not inside the corporation, thus limiting your potential for growth in the company. Do you think you do not have to be influenced by what your colleagues do? That you are self-confident enough to be able to take your own consumption decisions? Do not underestimate the influence of your environment in your decisions. The worst lie we can tell to ourselves is that if we earned more money, we would have more money.

If you want to be rich, work to learn and save money to create your own financial assets or to educate yourself according to the need of the moment. Do not get into debt to get more degrees. Sir Ken Robinson says that there exists degree inflation today[66]. The degrees on your résumé will only give you the illusion of being more employable, but they are not of real value. Do not forget that an MBA is an enormous liability.

You can learn by yourself by reading books, attending finance seminars, or looking for mentors who will teach you to invest. This will give you a real return on your investment. Begin there, and then decide if you still want to pursue an MBA.

This is what Tim Ferriss, author of the best seller *The Four-Hour Work Week*, did. After graduating from a prestigious college (Princeton) and feeling tempted by Stanford's MBA, his enthusiasm about an MBA degree went from the clouds to the ground in only one day. He attended a few "Entrepreneurship and Venture Capital" classes that were offered as a sampling of the program, with a few brilliant teachers who left him open-mouthed. In thirty minutes, he had learned more than he had from all of the books he had read on the topic. He was determined to take the plunge. Then he walked around the campus and slipped into some other classes, only to realize that the class that had left him open-mouthed was the exception to the rule. The rest of classes were about theoretical and soporific speculations of a few PhDs. This was the end of his MBA fever. He took the money he had for the MBA (around $120,000) and contacted some "business angels' who became his mentors. He invested his money in some start-ups with small amounts (around $20,000) with the goal being to learn. Within two years, he learned what he might never have learned at business school, and he even recovered part of his money.[67]

He also attended, on another occasion, a weekend conference led by Warren Buffet. He later declared that he had acquired in one weekend more than what he could have acquired by completing an MBA: real-world strategies proved by the experience of a genius and amazing networking. And in the process, he saved more than $100,000 and two years of his time.[68] Did you know that Buffett was not admitted into Harvard? Several billions of dollars later, most would agree that he did not need the Harvard brand to be successful.

The knowledge you can get with an MBA degree is not rare, inaccessible, or exclusive; it is just expensive, and its applications are not necessarily practical.

The MBA Bubble

Many people agree that the MBA is a bad investment, but only a few will dare to say it. One of them is University of New York professor Andrew Hacker, who is appalled by the disproportionate cost of MBA tuition.[69] He contends that today, more than ever, even those who have degrees from prestigious universities will remain in the middle class.[70]

There is a reason why only a few have the courage to criticize the value added by the MBA degree.

9
Why There Is So Little Criticism of the MBA

The important thing is the obvious thing nobody is saying.

William S. Burroughs, American Writer

I guess that, after having shared several chapters of this book with me, you already know me a little bit. Maybe you have realized that I like to say what I think. In fact, I cannot stand it if I am unable to say what I think. And I cannot stand those who try to censure others so that they can hear only what they want to hear. I do not deny it; this attitude has caused me some trouble, but freedom of expression is a noble value for me.

However, I spent ten years keeping the information in this book to myself, in spite of feeling that everyone who was considering an MBA should know it. Only if someone asked, I answered shyly that I had not valued the program much. Why do you think a big mouth like me was so hesitant to talk about the worst mistake of her career for so long? I did it for a simple reason that I share with all those who have an MBA: I am human.

You surely know the story of the emperor's new clothes. The story tells that a king was cheated by a few

The MBA Bubble

charlatans. They made him believe that they would make him a suit with magnificent fabric. This fabric would be invisible to the idiots. The king loved this idea so much that he accepted the deal. When his new suit was ready, the king was taken through the streets of the village with his new clothes, and all of the people admired his suit. Everyone was aware that the king had been told the fabric had extraordinary properties, so everyone said it was wonderful. Until a child, too young to understand the consequences of his words, shouted to the crowd, "The king is naked!"

Put yourself in that situation and, with a hand on your heart, tell me what would you have done if you had been there, in the Middle Ages, with no right to fair judgment and with the threat of torture as a punishment for insulting the king? Would you have shouted the truth to the wind? I must say that I would not have shouted it, nor whispered it, nor insinuated it. You probably would not have done it, either.

What is the moral of this story? That just because the whole world says that something is true does not mean that it really is. Think about it: Often the most frequent arguments are not the most logical.

I am not suggesting that all the MBA graduates think the same thing I do about their degree. But I do affirm that there are much more of them than there seem to be. It simply does not make any sense for them to talk about it, especially in an "official" way.

Why There Is So Little Criticism on the MBA

Nowadays, torture does not exist in our civilized societies, and everyone has the right to fair judgment on the west side of the world. Still, most people are extremely dependent on their aptitude to get a job in the best possible conditions. It makes no sense to say in a loud voice something that would put them at a disadvantage.

If they have spent a fortune in tuition and have lost one or two years of their lives in an effort that will hardly provide a differential to their career, it is difficult for them to admit that this differential is even less valued. Saying officially that they have made so much effort only to fill the pockets of business schools' shareholders is like shouting that the emperor is naked. They have to do what they can to try to get a return on their investment. For example, they may say at any opportunity they have that the program has provided a differential value to their careers. This way, if they are lucky, their employer will agree in sharing the perception of that value with them.

One of my MBA classmates, who was a father, thought the MBA degree was a bad investment. He said, "I spent a lot of money doing this master's…really a lot…and I am not going to get it back. But when they ask me what I think about the MBA, I am going to say that it has been the best thing I did in my life. I don't have any choice."

That's why I said nothing until I decided to leave the corporate world. It made no sense for me to say publicly what I am saying to you right now. And you

The MBA Bubble

can be sure that very few will dare to say it, even in a low voice, though they may think it. Nobody likes to take the risk of looking like an idiot for saying that the king is naked or of taking the risk of being judged by the king. Most people prefer to make the effort to believe that the king's clothes are magnificent. I have not been the exception until now.

For people who depend on the corporate world for their living, there are risks that it does not make any sense to take. Why would they say something that might harm them?

It is a paradox. Many of us applied to an MBA program to have more options and to have better careers. But after graduating, we realized that we are weaker than those who did not pursue the degree.

So maybe at this point you agree with me that there is a good reason why most people avoid criticizing the program. But some people do say what they think. I am not a lonely prophet.

One of these solitary riders is Henry Mintzberg, who does not have an MBA but knows a lot about it because he was an MBA professor until he decided to quit. He did not agree with what was being taught in the program anymore. In his book *Managers, Not MBAs*,[71] he criticizes explicitly the dysfunctional management education given in the MBA program to people who do not have any managerial experience. Mintzberg points an accusing finger at both business schools, with their corrupt marketing, and at graduates for the greed that attracted them to business schools' promises. His book serves as a prediction of the horrible crisis of 2008 because it describes the consequences for society of the attitudes inculcated at business schools.

Tim Ferriss, author of the best seller *The Four-Hour Work Week*,[72] also questions openly the value added by an MBA, especially in comparison to its alternatives. He does not come to the point of affirming that it is better to stay home reading a couple of books in your pyjamas, but he does affirm that it is possible to obtain a high-class education without plunging into the "eighty-hour-work-week-depressing-job" lifestyle. He contends in his book that it is not necessary to have a degree from a prestigious school to be able to finance the lifestyle you want. "There are unrecognized benefits to not coming out of [a top academic institution]. How do I know? I've been there and seen the destruction." I have also seen it.

Probably the most explicit flag bearer of the anti-MBA message is Josh Kaufman, author of the best seller *The Personal MBA*.[73] His book and his manifesto[74] provide evidence of the senseless waste of money and energy based on the limited benefits provided by the program. By the time Kaufman got a job as an assistant brand manager at Procter & Gamble, he had read hundreds of business books. This self-education allowed him to be able to discuss topics at the same level as his MBA colleagues. Kaufman considered the possibility of plunging into the program but he quickly realized that he would hang to his neck a heavy load—a colossal

The MBA Bubble

debt that would take decades to pay back, only to obtain a job like the one he already had in a big corporation, one he might not be able to escape. This had no sense when he realized that corporate life was made him definitely unhappy. That's how he decided to start his own business project and write his book, turning into entrepreneur to work in his own terms.

The catalyst of his project was a post on Seth Godin's blog. Godin is a brilliant author and marketing guru, and he has a fancy Stanford MBA degree. While the mass media was scandalized by the debate on the ethics of a few applicants to Harvard's MBA program who tried to hack the Harvard system to know if they had been admitted, Godin had a very different vision. Instead of being infuriated, he suggested that Harvard had given them good news and had done them a favor by not admitting them. In turning them down, the school actually returned to them two years of their lives and $150,000.[75] Indeed, when I see it with perspective, I realize that my school would have given me a great gift if they had not admitted me. Seth Godin regrets it as much as I do, and he finds it hard to understand why people continue believing that obtaining a piece of paper is a better use of their time and money than real experience combined with the dedicated reading of thirty or forty books. In fact, he launched a challenging offer to his readers: "Do not go to business school."[76] Instead, he advised people to engage in six months of free learning with him. In that program, participants could discuss business topics with him and with other brilliant twenty-first-century business gurus.

Why There Is So Little Criticism on the MBA

My favorite MBA critic is the most acid of all. I am talking about Dilbert, the great star of the American comic that portrays life in the office. "I have an MBA from a *top* business school. I am a management expert because I read case studies of businesses that were in completely different situations. Wait a minute. Why does this suddenly seem ridiculous?" a Dilbert's colleague says. And the parodies continue in the comic strip: "I hear you have an MBA, just like the jerks who ruined the economy." Or this ironic comment from Dilbert's boss, which reflects so well the way companies value these degrees: "Congratulations to my secretary, Carol, for getting her MBA. In this company, we believe that hard work should be rewarded. Next time you fetch my coffee, get some coffee for yourself, too."

In addition to all of these known MBA critics, hundreds of anonymous critics take part in forums and articles, making comments with indignation. Hundreds more claim their indignation behind closed doors in the business schools' career services offices, only to realize that they are powerless against the system. I was not surprised when, as I conducted research for this book, I came across the story of the "revolt" of several MBA students from one of the most prestigious European business schools. They realized that what they were expecting from the MBA degree did not have a counterpart in the reality of the market.

Unfortunately for all those who will come after them, very few will dare to talk, and almost none will do it in a loud voice. Most of them will get used to having the degree on their résumés as soon as the storm passes. They will find a good job after making a lot of effort, as I did, and they will get acclimated to the new reality. They would have found a job anyway with the same effort but no degree, but now they have a pretty and sophisticated decoration on their résumés, and they will forget their indignation. After all, an MBA is almost always valued as positive, although there is a huge gap between its price and its value.

And in this way, the cycle continues. The system continues working. The business schools' marketing voices are more effective, more frequent, more camouflaged and have a better reputation than the few rebels who have the guts to question the degree's value. However, the opposite is also true. It has been ten years since I got my degree, and I have hardly heard anyone defending the program, apart from those who are involved in the business of business schools.

I am not saying there are no satisfied graduates—people who value what the MBA has given to them and think it was a good decision. On the contrary, often their smiling faces appear in business schools' marketing leaflets. But where can unsatisfied graduates express themselves except in some anonymous forum?

You are not likely to hear the opinions of many disappointed MBA graduates, nor are you likely to learn what percentage of all MBA graduates they represent. But it is significant.

Why There Is So Little Criticism on the MBA

By now, you have heard some strong arguments that question the MBA's value. But why do business schools still have so many customers if an MBA adds eventually so little value?

10
Why Do Business Schools Still Have Customers?

Whenever you find yourself on the side of the majority, it is time to pause and reflect.

Mark Twain

If the price of a company's shares increases constantly, it is often a sign of its success and the quality of its products or services, do you agree? Well, often it is, but not always.

I am going to tell you a story about a great company, an admired company that *Fortune* magazine rewarded for five consecutive years for being the most innovative company. It became one of the seven biggest companies in the United States. Its executive director held an MBA from Harvard. The price of the company's shares increased constantly for many years, as if the company were increasing the value to shareholders.

It actually wasn't. Enron's shares dwindled, in little more than one year, from $90 to less than $1, and its bankruptcy turned into the worst managerial fraud in history.

Sometimes there are reasons for a price increase other than an increase in the added value. In fact, price is a direct consequence of the law of supply and demand, so if demand increases, so does price. But this demand increase is not always reasonable. Here are some examples of this concept:

- Houses were overvalued in Spain in 2006. Yet real estate demand was increasing in a constant manner.

- Though many "dot com" companies did not have a sustainable business model, many of them were bought for millions of dollars before 2001.

- Anyone can cultivate tulips in Holland, but in 1637, a bulb cost more than a house on an Amsterdam channel.

Real value and price are not always correlated. Instead, price and demand are (given that supply remains pretty constant). But demand does not necessarily increase after a rational, meticulous, and deep analysis of the intrinsic value of the good or product. Often, demand is a function of the *expectation* of an increase in future value or a positive return on investment of the good or product, although this expectation has been formed in an irrational way.

This is known as the "bubble effect."

Why Do Business Schools Still Have Customers?

In a bubble, the price of the good or product in question does not stop growing, and this raise turns into the justification for a demand increase, so prices rise even more. Being intelligent will not protect you from falling into the trap of a bubble. Even geniuses have been trapped. Isaac Newton, a brilliant man, lost thousands of pounds with the shares of the South See Company in the eighteenth century.

The big problem with bubbles is that the whole world agrees on their existence when they burst, but not when they are producing. However, some indicators make it possible to detect financial bubbles:

- There is an accepted, widespread, and rarely analyzed opinion about the return on investment for a good or product. For example, "House prices never decrease" or "Getting an MBA implies a significant salary increase." I call this "collective irrationality."

- The investments of the bubble begin to be financed by bank loans.

- There is a bad assignment of resources. For example, more houses are constructed than are needed to shelter the population, or there are more MBA graduates than the market demands.[77]

- Prices and supply in a market are much higher than the historical value of such good or products.

The parallelism between what is happening in the business-school sector and what has happened in the economy is chilling. MBA tuition has increased an average of 62 percent since 2005.[78] Isn't that troubling?

The increase in MBA demand is due to an education bubble, or an unreal *expectation* of the return on investment of the programs, not to real added value.

What can increase the expectation of the ROI of an MBA? Well, do not forget that an investment is analyzed against its alternative. Many factors can influence the perception of the difference between getting an MBA and not getting it. *Perception, not reality.* I know the difference by experience. Do you have any idea what influences this perception?

- The "financial academic engineering" of the rankings of business schools shows growth in average wages that is questioned even by business schools themselves.

- The stability of the labor market has constantly degraded in the last twenty years, favoring the idealization of the degree as a refuge. We have inherited this belief from former middle-class generations, which believed that a formal education was a guarantee of prosperity and wealth.

- The labor experience has become less and less satisfactory and turns out to be a source of alienation. Many people see the MBA as a way to change careers.

- Business schools' marketing focuses on inflating the perception of graduates' potential for employability and the degree's ability to open the door for the best jobs, creating the illusion that if one does not have the degree, he or she is out of the party.

- The competitive MBA admission process creates the illusion of an exclusive and elitist reward that is attainable for only a few.

- Banks have favored the financing of an MBA degree almost with no other prerequisites than admission to a business school.

That's it. A bubble grows when people give away reason and prudence in favour of hope and greed.

The truth is that most of those who apply to MBA programs have unrealistic expectations of the value they are going to get with the program. If they are unemployed and they want to get an MBA with the expectation that it will help them get a job, that's a bad thing. If they want to change industries or functions, it's also a bad thing. If they want to increase their salary in the short term, it's a bad thing. Some people argue that the program's results are seen in the long term. No, long-term results are the fruit of one's own effort, so one had better follow the program for other reasons. As for the argument that an MBA increases employability, well, it does, but in a really marginal way, whereas the personal and financial effort that is required is enormous. The degree does not justify itself.

I have already talked to you about many of these false expectations, and I will talk later on about some I have not mentioned yet. But the truth is that they are only expectations. They are not the rational consequence of a deep value analysis.

Try Not to Be the Greatest Fool of All

The bubbles and their causes have not been completely explained, but there is a theory that seems funny to me, and it is the theory of the "greater fool".

According to this theory, a few perennially optimistic participants in the market (the fools) buy overvalued assets expecting a high ROI. The bubble will continue growing while there are greater fools who believe that their ROI will be high until the greatest fools of all remain stuck with assets they bought at astronomical prices because nobody wants them.

Why Do Business Schools Still Have Customers?

I regret having to admit that I have been the greatest fool of all, and many of us are the greatest fools who have invested in an MBA believing we would get a return on our investment but did not. The MBA is a not even an asset that we can sell to recover part of the loss; it is only a piece of paper that the market scarcely values.

Every MBA candidate who follows the program believing he or she will obtain a value that does not materialize is the greatest fool of all in this game. But you can be saved if you identify and anticipate the end of the bubble before it comes or avoid entering the game.

First of all, I will ask you to exercise good skepticism. Even if you do not question the accuracy of the wage information published by business schools in the rankings, tell me what logic you find in the fact that MBA wages have increased in the last years. Do not forget that salary is nothing more than the result of the demand and supply law game in the labor market. I do not see an increased demand for MBA professionals when the labor market has been depressed for at least five years, constantly degrading—yet MBA programs' offers do nothing but grow.

On the other hand, the beginning of the end of a bubble is marked by the deceleration of the demand, and it is already happening. The Graduate Management Admission Council (GMAC) application trend survey report for 2011 reveals that 67 percent of business schools showed a decrease in their applications for the two-year-program and 57 percent show a decrease in applications to the one-year program, whereas in 2010, application growth was still positive.[79] Even the most prestigious schools like Stanford, Harvard, and Wharton have noticed the trend.

This illusion cannot last forever. It does not seem logical to me that brilliant young people can continue to believe that they have to thank business schools for "allowing" them to pay a fortune in tuition and to give up two years of their lives in exchange for a piece of paper. It seems incredible that people ask more questions before buying car insurance than before getting an MBA, as if they had forgotten at some point that they are the customers.

11
The Magic Moment when You Forgot That You Are the Customer

A common mistake is to believe that the one who has more customers is the most skillful.

Denis Diderot, French Philosopher and Writer

Many people consider themselves to be demanding customers. I do. When you buy something, you probably expect quality and service. You've earned your money with a lot of effort, so you want to be completely satisfied with the product you are going to buy. You want to exert your power as a consumer.

Except with the MBA degree.

In that case, the norm is not fulfilled, and you behave like the most obedient of the sheeps in the flock, giving away all your money in the moment business school tells you to do so, thanking God, Holy Mary, Buddha, Allah, or whoever because they let you become a customer.

Business schools' admission process has not only the effect of shortlisting candidates who will guarantee the success of the school (sorry—I mean "who have the aptitude to complete the program successfully," according to the official version); it also generates a fictitious feeling of scarcity, totally opposite the feeling of abundance that is generated in an ordinary purchase process.

In the case of the MBA degree, you compete to be able to buy something, and only 10, 20, or 30 percent of the candidates accede to the "exclusive" right of becoming customers. In the meantime, many of them forget to evaluate what they are buying thoroughly. That's what happened to Joe Mihalic, the Harvard MBA graduate who was consumed by debt,[80] and it happened to me.

Getting admitted to an MBA program is a long process. The effort required to apply and to pass the Graduate Management Admission Test (GMAT) or equivalent exam is enormous. It can take months or even years to prepare yourself. You will need to study a lot for your GMAT and perhaps take a course to prepare for it. You will need to gather recommendation letters and write some essays. In addition to all that, you will need to study all of the information available on the school of your dreams to convince them that you are in love with the institution, which hopefully will increase your chance of being admitted. Intuitively you know that if the school's admissions team has doubts about your willing to be a flag bearer of their brand for the rest of your life, they will not admit you. You have to make them believe that they can take the credit for your success forever. So you study the script and you end up picturing yourself in the role of MBA student. In the

The Magic Moment when You Forgot That You Are the Customer

end, you end up selling yourself on the institution you want to "buy."

While you are participating in this circus, it is normal that you forget that you are the one who wants to buy, not the one who wants to sell. The day you receive a letter from the school, you will feel a knot in your stomach. Will you be among the exclusive 10 percent to have the honor to spend a fortune in tuition and be buried in debt for a decade? Slowly you open your letter, and...you have been admitted! *Oh, thank you, thank you Youvegotme business school! Thank you for admitting me! I am one of the chosen to belong to the elite and privileged ones who will work as slaves for years, only to pay back a huge debt!*

It did not sound so ridiculous to me at that moment, but it would have been convenient if it had because that was the magic moment in which I forgot that I was the customer. In fact, as soon as I received the letter, I ran out to thank those who had helped me with the admission process. And I was never again a customer of the business school. The only moment in which I had the power to check what I was buying, the power to be a demanding customer of the business school, had passed by quickly.

By the moment the program had begun, I had to pay the totality of tuition. I would never have the right to have the basic guarantee—"satisfied or you will have your money back"—that is a part of just about any independent training offer today. In fact, traditional

The MBA Bubble

Business Schools will have to soon face a reality they never thought they would be confronted with— "real life" competitors as Qopolis Business School[81], which is a 100% cloud-based University. Qopolis University will provide world class business training imparted by "real world" business people, experienced in building multi-million dollar companies and being successful in the real world outside of academia, starting January 2014. The application fee will be only US $7 to all students around the world. Their value proposition includes 2 Money Back Guarantees. First, there is a 130-day Tuition Refund Guarantee. If the student is in any way unhappy or not satisfied after the first semester, Qopolis guarantees to return 100% of the tuition. Second, for all graduating students of the 120-credit hour Bachelors of Business Development degree program, Qopolis will return 100% of a student's tuition at graduation, so that everybody graduates without tuition debt. They will teach all the students over 50 ways to make money during the first semester so that students can make money and not be in debt after college. If I were a very demanding customer with my education as I was with anything else, it would have been obvious to me by seeing this value proposition that traditional business schools are far from having an attractive offer.

The very moment you "buy an MBA," you stop being the customer. Once you are admitted, the business school reps are no longer interested in your satisfaction, even if they may pretend they are. Josh Kaufman, author of *The Personal MBA*,[82] does not mince words: "If you are successful in the years after graduation, the

The Magic Moment when You Forgot That You Are the Customer

school will hold you up as a shining example of the quality of their program and will use the 'halo' effect. If you lose your job and go broke, you'll get neither publicity nor help, but the loan bills will keep rolling in. Sorry about your luck." It describes exactly my own experience, both the bad and good times. It became so evident (and insulting) while I followed the program that it is hard for me to believe that, as Kaufman says, this is a common reality of all business schools and not a weakness of mine.

Kaufman is not the only one who speaks out. Seth Godin affirms that colleges, like airports, see their customers as transients without power who will be gone tomorrow while they will continue to be there.[83]

This should not be surprising. This is a common occurrence when you leave behind the marketing portals that lured you there. In his book,[84] Philip Delves Broughton tells an anecdote of a Harvard MBA student who said to a business school's administrative employee, "Why are you treating me like this? I am the customer, goddammit," to which the employee answered, "No, you are not. You're the product." With much less dissimulation of an anonymous anecdote, the dean of Dartmouth stated in an article published in the 1980s, "Business schools are bottling plants. The product is 90 percent finished before coming here. We put it in a bottle and label it."[85]

It seems more and more surprising that brilliant people with high potential surrender obediently to a system that does not add any practical value to them but costs the sacrifice of the best years of their lives. I would not have done it if I had realized how the system works. Many people think the fact that business schools are expensive employment agencies justifies the effort. But they do not consider you a customer even when they help you find a job.

The director of the careers services center at my school, the one who was responsible for fulfilling the highest expectation of the students as customers, seemingly was measured in his functions only by the percentage of graduates who got a job after graduation and for the percentage who got those jobs through the school. The quality of the job or the conditions in which students had to work was not his business. Without even pretending about the incongruity with regard to the marketing messages, he encouraged us to accept any type of offer, even if it was in a lower category than our previous jobs. He was not even bothering to conceal his disinterest for the students. Once he entered the room where we were working as a team and threw us out of there, saying "Get out of here, you scum." I do not remember if he had the right to throw us out or not, but I felt that his behavior was in poor taste. He was Spanish, and my Spanish colleagues told me that it was a cultural thing, a very Spanish kind of humor. Even though I had lived in Spain for seven years and enjoyed the Spanish good humor, I could not understand what was so funny. Some time later, another Spanish professor made this confession to me: "If I were a student today and if I listened to what X says, I would feel insulted." Well, I felt insulted. But it was already

The Magic Moment when You Forgot That You Are the Customer

too late to complain. I was not a customer anymore, I was chopped meat.

I continue thinking that this was a weakness of my school and that not all MBA students are treated like that. But the nonchalance of one person, who is still in the same position, by the way, demonstrates something—that the industry of business schools can ignore customer satisfaction for years and it will not affect them. The reality is that *people, as soon as they become students, are not customers anymore.* Customers are those who the business schools will pursue, those they need to convince to apply and to pay tuition. Students and graduates, in any case, will attract more customers if they are satisfied and will shut up if they are not. This is the way the system works.

The truth is that even though some schools attract prestigious employers by the power of their brands, it will always be your own responsibility to find a job, and you will have to make the same effort as if you didn't have the degree. You will have to compete with other candidates who can get the attention of the same companies, and you will not have any advantage by holding an MBA, even if it was easier for you to get an interview. On the contrary, you will be two years older than your competitors or you will have two years' less professional experience.

You will have successes in your professional career; I do not have any doubt about it. If you have been admitted to a business school, it's because they have guarantees of your capacities. But your success will be the consequence of your sweat and not of the MBA. You could have sweated without mortgaging your future. You also could have gotten the same results without letting an educational institution use your achievements to fill fancy leaflets and take the credit for them.

You will never care again about the marketing speech you have heard for the last few years. Nobody will care what the position of your school in the rankings is. Smart people who work hard are successful with or without an MBA. Remember the words of Stanford's professor, Jeffrey Pfeffer: "If you have the talent to get in, you can succeed regardless." And while the MBA is a nice decoration on your résumé, it is not what will make a company marry you. First they will weigh many other characteristics that you can develop and that will make you pass other candidates, even those with an MBA from a top-ranked school.

But there are exceptions. Some people (not many) get a real value from their MBA program. I will talk about this at the end of the book. But almost none of them recognize that they have power as customers.

Let me tell you a story about the importance of not forgetting who the customer is. It is the story of a French colleague I knew in my last corporate adventure. Just like me, he reached a point at which corporate life began to be unbearable, and he decided to launch his own business. He had great success, considering that he did not invest too much money. One

The Magic Moment when You Forgot That You Are the Customer

year later and with only one employee, his company multiplied its value by twenty times. Not bad. He deserves applause. Suddenly, managing the growth of his company became complicated. He needed to acquire new competences. His decision? To train himself, to get an MBA from one of the most prestigious European business schools based in Paris (probably a good decision in his case; I will talk about this at the end of the book). Taking into account his potential and what he had already demonstrated, he was admitted immediately. But he did something entirely different than most applicants do (including me): As soon as he was admitted, he positioned himself as a customer and negotiated a 50 percent discount in tuition.

Do as he did. Do not forget that you are the customer. If you decide that the MBA is really what you need, even after my discouraging you that it is not, you have some time between the moment when you are admitted and the moment when you reserve your seat. It is possible that applications are decreasing and that you can negotiate the tuition. Maybe they will not accept your offer, but you have the power to try. Maybe you will be surprised. However, if getting an MBA is really what you want, do it tactfully. Business schools are very haughty, and the move can be dangerous. Also, that is the moment to ask all the questions you want; it will be too late once you have paid your tuition. Do not forget it: *Caveat emptor*, a powerful Latin phrase that means you must check what you are buying or you will not have the right to your money back later.

The MBA Bubble

Do not be swayed by business schools' marketing speeches. Do not believe everything they say to you. Do your work as a consumer. If your expectation is to get a salary increase, go to LinkedIn or Facebook and find at least three people who have gone to the school that you want to go and ask them if they think the salary increase you want to obtain after completing your MBA degree is logical. In addition, ask if they think the increase would be obtained because of the MBA (and especially in today's tough economy) and not to the normal evolution of your career. Try to find at least three people who confirm to you that your expectation is realistic and that there is a high probability of obtaining what you want, whether you want to get a higher salary, change industries, enter management, or increase your employability.

When asking, ensure that you formulate your questions properly. Do not ask about the salary of the person in question, but on his or her opinion about the market, with precise numbers. People can be shy about discussing their own incomes. Ask for their opinions about the accuracy of the average wages published in the rankings and about the possibility of obtaining the above- mentioned wage increase as a result of completing the MBA. Remember—*correlation is not equal to causality.* Formulate the questions in a way that will not cause you to come to the erroneous conclusion that you will obtain a certain level of salary as a consequence of getting an MBA. Do not ask vaguely if the person is satisfied with his or her MBA; be specific with your questions. Most people will say that they have appreciated the program, but it does not

The Magic Moment when You Forgot That You Are the Customer

mean that the investment in time and money is worth it. Do not forget that you are buying something that you will never be able to return, with a very long payback time. Really long.

Speak also with the Human Resources specialists in your company. Ask them to what extent they think the MBA adds value. But ask them in depth. Everybody (even me) will say to you that the program is valued on your résumé, but *that does not mean it is worth effort and cost*. Investigate the differential value; you will probably discover that it is minimal. Are there any successful people without an MBA in your company? How did they get there?

If you speak with someone about a company that interests you and you feel that you have a good chance of working there, and the person says to you that an MBA is highly valued in the company, put things into perspective. Does it mean the MBA will be profitable for you or that it will be profitable only for the company because you will work as a slave? Is it the only company to which you can postulate? Often, the best chance of profitability for you is not where the whole world is competing, but where there is less competition. Look for the companies where you can compete better according to your qualifications. In many successful companies, no one has an MBA. Apple is one of them, and it is far from being the only one. Many highly profitable and unknown companies pay excellent wages and do not have last-century requirements.

Let me give you some advice: Look for information in forums, but do not put too much trust in them. A lot of people say something without having any idea what they are saying. I also suspect that many of the comments are nothing more than disguised marketing messages from business schools. I assure you that false comments in forums are a part of the marketing strategy of almost any company, regardless of its reputation. In fact, there was a scandal a few years ago between two prestigious French business schools. One of them was suspected of having organized a campaign to discredit the other one in a very popular student forum[86]. Look for the opinion of "real people." If more than one "real" person says the same thing to you, take their opinion seriously.

And finally, as soon as you are satisfied with your realistic vision of the value contributed by an MBA program, it will be time to evaluate your investment in contrast to the alternatives. Effectiveness is not the same thing as efficiency. You can kill flies with cannon shots or use insecticide. Both may be effective, but only one is efficient. Are you sure that the most effective, efficient, and profitable way to meet your professional goals is to buy a piece of paper at an astronomical price?

12
Recognize Your Professional Goals First

Strategy without tactics is the slowest route to victory. Tactics without strategy is noise before defeat.

Sun Tzu

It is sad, but many MBA applicants pursue the degree for the wrong reasons. I did it for the wrong reasons, and I was not the only one.

When I say "wrong reasons," I do not mean that the applicants are not necessarily going to meet their professional goals but that the MBA is not the ideal accelerator to reach them, nor is it the most profitable path. In the following chapters of this book, I am going to show you that there are almost always more effective and profitable ways of meeting your goals. The MBA may look like the fast track, but it is not.

Let's be honest. What most people look for when getting an MBA is better jobs and higher salaries, although they do not specify how the MBA will help them reach those goals. A higher salary was not exactly what I was looking for, but it seemed to be an inherent benefit of getting the degree, and it was one of the major expectations of most of my classmates. Who doesn't want to earn more money?

Some other people get an MBA mainly because of fear. They want to protect themselves from the degradation of the labor market. They have the illusion of being more employable with the degree. They hope that the nice piece of paper certifies that they belong to an elite club of people who have been trained in a few exceptional skills demanded by the market.

Others want, in a less precise way, to "improve their long-term career progression." What exactly do they mean? Not all of them know. They feel that an MBA must be something good for their career. And nobody seems to say the opposite, after all.

Others want to project themselves into the international market and seek to become employed in a certain country. That was the case for me, and today it is the case for many applicants who go to study in the United States or in northern European countries looking for better economic opportunities.

Others, not many, have a real motivation for learning new abilities that could improve their careers. But most of them do not know what those abilities are or why the market might value them.

Others want to know extraordinary people who will forever provide access to the best professional opportunities.

Recognize Your Professional Goals First

Others want to change their day-to-day reality and be able to leave their boring and meaningless jobs. They want to find new horizons by changing industries or job functions. They want to escape, to return to college time, and to return with a stronger foothold in the professional world.

Many have unconscious goals that are implicit in their decision, but they are unable to articulate those goals. Some of them want to be more self-confident, and they think their professional value will be certified by a fancy degree. Some want to look important in the eyes of others or want their parents to feel proud of them or want recognition from their colleagues and bosses. That is the secret, unconscious, and unrecognized dream of many MBA applicants. Although it is a silent motivation, it is often the most important one that some people make at the critical moment of making the decision to apply. Emotion is one of the most important elements of any decision in life.

Most MBA applicants share more than one of the previous motivations, and they form a dangerous combination that can cause them to make wrong decisions, as I did.

The Worst Mistake You Can Make

The worst mistake you can make at the moment of applying to an MBA program is *not being specific* about what you want to obtain from the program and about how an MBA will help you get it. Often those who consider applying make the decision too fast. They also spend too much time deciding which school they should choose, asking here and there, looking at leaflets and surfing the web and the forums. But they do not have a precise idea of why they want to get an MBA. Their reasoning is vague, as in "It certainly has a positive impact on people's careers, doesn't it? If it were a bad idea, business schools would not have customers."

That's not a good start. *Be specific*. Why do you want to get an MBA? What are the specific results you expect from following the program, which will cost you a fortune and demand an extraordinary effort?

In his book *Managers, Not MBAs*,[87] Mintzberg tells the anecdote of the son of a friend who came to him to ask for advice on which school to choose. The boy had already made the decision to get an MBA. When the author suggested that he should strengthen his experience in an industry that interests him first instead of doing an MBA, the boy's eyes glazed over. He seemed to be upset by the answer. However, another boy Mintzberg advised took his words into account. Even though he was admitted to a good business school, he decided not to enter the program. He got a new job he loves and is learning a lot—with no debt. This story demonstrates the value of asking yourself the important questions first.

You should spend much more time answering the question of why you want to get an MBA. Few applicants spend enough time doing this. The "brand" of the product you choose is secondary. You should know first if the product that you are going to buy is what you need.

The Truth About Wages

If you want to get an MBA, it is possible that you share a common expectation with most MBA applicants: You want to earn more. You probably want to have a better salary and better benefits. You look at what you earn every month, and it seems to be not enough. The ways of making it increase seem to be remote. Suddenly a leaflet from a fancy business school lands in your hands. It makes you believe an MBA is a ticket to top managerial positions...with better wages! It seems possible that it is the easiest path to meet your goals, which seem to be unattainable otherwise.

Some job-market experts do not agree with what your leaflets say. Christian Bang Rouhet, a former human resources director of a big multinational corporation with many years of experience in human resources consultancy, believes that before getting an MBA, it is necessary to evaluate the program's ROI closely. He says that a salary increase is not always a direct consequence of an MBA degree. That's why what applicants should look for is for the coherence of the degree in the evolution of the professional project.

I invite you to leave behind the paradigms of your childhood. When you were a child and you accomplished an extraordinary achievement such as

The MBA Bubble

winning a competition or doing extra work at home, everyone gave you compliments. Your parents may have even given you a gift to reward your efforts.

But the labor market does not work this way. No one is going to give you compliments because you have made more effort or because you accomplished something extraordinary like getting a fancy degree. No company is going to give you a supplementary penny because you have a nice piece of paper if they do not think that it is going to have a significant impact on their bottom line or that it adds value to the company.

The labor market works according to the law of supply and demand. Having an MBA does not change that fact. As an employee, you are an expense for a company. Therefore, a company will try to pay you the lowest possible salary. *If you can make an impact on a company's bottom line, if you add value in a way not many people can, and if you can prove it, you might earn a higher salary.* It is simple as that.

If you want to earn more, you should wonder: *How do I increase the value I provide in a unique way?*

Please do not respond by saying you will get an MBA. Remember—*be specific.*

If you add a lot of value but many other people can add the same value as you for less money, you are not indispensable, even if you have an MBA. Your salary will not increase. If you have a few uncommon abilities

Recognize Your Professional Goals First

(for example, you speak Hebrew), but you can't find anybody to whom this could add any value, you will not become a high-value, high-salary resource. Do you follow me?

The cruel reality is that many people have an MBA nowadays, and it is not clear how a young professional in his twenties without any management experience will be able to add more value to a company just because he has read five hundred business cases for which he has postulated top management decisions.

In my opinion, the only supplementary value the MBA adds is to "certify" that you are smart and trained to work as a slave. But is it the only way you have of demonstrating that you are smart and that you can work hard?

There Are More Profitable Ways

Think about it for a moment. What is the most difficult characteristic for a company to find in an employee?

Specialized experience. If a company wants to develop a new market, it will look for employees who have experience and strategic knowledge in that market. Management will be willing to pay more to them because they add significant value.

Maybe you are employed in an industry that is laying off employees or relocating its business, and therefore you do not see any possibility of increasing your value in the market. The MBA may appear to be a good means of changing industries. But I have already demonstrated that it is not easier to change industries with an MBA than it is to do so without it. Both ways, you will have to fight.

If you really want to change industries, you will have to employ a specific strategy. First choose the industry in which you would like to work. Think about an industry that has constant growth and evolves continuously. Consider the long term. This preparation will be the most critical of your career.

Then contact people who are employed in that industry. You can find them by identifying the companies that are growing in that industry and looking for persons on social media sites who are employed there. Contact them. Some of them will not answer you, but you may be surprised at how open some people are to helping you in your career. Tell them your intentions and ask their opinion for how you might enter the industry. Persevere. It may take one or two years, but finally an opportunity will show up. When you get one, you most likely will not earn a high salary in the beginning. You can even expect to have a slightly lower salary than what you are earning now. But by taking that route instead of pursuing an MBA degree, you will save a fortune in tuition. You also will have found the key to providing value to other companies in the same industry. Even the company that hires you might be willing to increase your salary to retain you if the market is growing.

Recognize Your Professional Goals First

Take courses in skills that the industry is demanding. Ask people who are in that industry if the training is likely to be useful; do not rely only on the opinion of the institution that wants to sell you the training. Seek to acquire abilities that you know the market is demanding. That is how you can invest in your career in a clever way.

Keep focused on your strategic long-term vision. Do not become a resource that increases its price under a "bubble effect". If that industry sector degenerates and the bubble explodes, your source of income will be seriously affected. Become a resource that adds value to the market in a sustainable way.

How to Grow in Your Current Company

You have probably heard the saying "Better the devil you know than the devil you don't." If you are also the angel your company knows well, there is a risk for them that you will leave to work for the competition. If that were to happen, your company might be willing to increase your salary to retain you because of the value you provide.

Remember the law of supply and demand. In a depressed market, if you leave and there are fifty candidates as good as you are who are willing to do your work for half the salary, the finance guys will not allow your boss to increase your salary, even if they value you as person. Do not force the negotiation against yourself.

You can also climb the corporate ladder in your organization. New responsibilities and abilities will make your salary increase over time. But before attempting that climb, ask yourself if it is what you really want. Being a manager could compromise your quality of life more than enhancing it.

To become a manager, you must have a certain degree of ambition and a natural need for power. I know the word "power" can have negative connotations, but it can be a positive attribute. Leaders like Nelson Mandela had a significant need for power. That's why he could defeat his enemies to change the world. Do you feel a need for power? If the answer is yes, then you probably have what it takes to move up in the hierarchy of your organization. If you also have leadership qualities, you have the aptitude to influence people positively. You do not need to learn this at business school because it is more of an art than a science; it cannot be learned in a classroom. I do not feel a need of power and the MBA did not change that.

In an excellent article in the *Harvard Business Review*, Anne Kreamer, former vice president at Nickelodeon, describes how she lost all interest in her work at her new position. She asks, "What if you do not want to be manager?"[88] Make sure you have a good answer for this question before you start climbing. If you don't, you risk making a lot of effort to climb a ladder that is standing against the wrong wall.

If, on the other hand, you want to evolve toward positions of higher responsibility that do not involve management functions, you will still have to master political skills. You will have to be able to identify those who have the power to impact your professional career and what they want in exchange. Read Machiavelli's *The Prince*. Then add to its political lessons a big dose of human values. Understand how decisions are made in your company. Cultivate the attitudes that powerful people value in an effort to position yourself to be promoted. Become a valuable right-hand person for them.

That is how people evolve in organizations. Political skills are a requirement for corporate growth. Those who grow, even if they are not conscious of it, earn the favors and confidence of those who make decisions. According to Richard Vacher, a senior expert in outplacement and the labor market, those who are protected from tough times are not necessarily the most competent but those who stand out in terms of their political skills. I do not mean that it is possible to be incompetent and successful because it is evident that if you do not do your work right, nobody will protect you in the long term. But even if you are the best in the world in your line of work, you will not grow without the favors of those whose decisions can impact your career.

If you do not feel comfortable engaging in corporate politics, you will not grow (or even remain) in an organization, even if you have an MBA from a top school. On the contrary, if you are excellent at politics, you likely will pass ahead of all your colleagues with MBAs. There is nothing wrong with having good political skills. I have known people with strong human values who have evolved by doing good work and being excellent at positioning themselves inside the organization. That was not the case for me, and my MBA did not change that. The need to position myself for a promotion distracted me from my work, and that is why I decided to leave the corporate world. But I do not think that there is anything intrinsically negative about being effective at politics. Those are the rules of the game—you play or you don't. And if you want to win, you need to follow the rules.

But you may be thinking that in today's tough times, the important thing is not to earn more but simply to have a good job. Maybe your job is at risk or you are unemployed. Maybe you think that although an MBA is bloody expensive, it is a requirement to access the best jobs in the market. You may think that if you do not have an MBA, you will be at a disadvantage compared to the thousands of other candidates who are fighting for the same jobs.

You may assume that an MBA will improve your employability. But, isn't that just a myth?

13
The MBA and the Employability Myth

Fanaticism consists in redoubling your effort when you have forgotten your aim.

George Santayana, Hispanic-American Philosopher and Writer

I am going to begin this chapter admitting it: An MBA adds value to a résumé. The MBA always looks good. Between two candidates who offer a comparable value, most companies will choose the one who has an MBA.

You may be thinking, *That's it. It is confirmed*—an MBA improves employability.

Yes, an MBA improves employability.

Is that all? This chapter ends here?

Of course not. Even though an MBA degree can improve employability, it is nonsense to complete an MBA degree in an effort to improve employability.

The Relationship Between Effort and Results

143

The MBA Bubble

Imagine that I sell you a method to lose weight. And I tell you that it works. You buy it, and after starving for four months, you manage to lose only one pound. Basically, I have not lied to you. You have lost weight with my method. But the results you have obtained did not compensate your effort, and it would have been more sensible for you to follow your usual diet.

Likewise, pursuing an MBA is not the most sensible way to set yourself apart in the marketplace. Knowing that the MBA improves employability it is not the most important thing. The most important thing is to know *how much* the degree improves employability, at what price, and if there are alternative ways to improve it with less effort.

I want to tell you about Pareto's law. Vilfredo Pareto was an Italian economist in the nineteenth century who observed that the distribution of almost everything in life corresponded to the rule of 80/20. For example, 20 percent of the population holds 80 percent of the wealth; Also, 20 percent of customers generate 80 percent of the benefits. And 20 percent of one's efforts generate 80 percent of the results.

> *"According to Pareto's law, 20 percent of ones efforts generate 80 percent of the results."*

It also works the other way around: Sometimes, 80 percent of one's efforts generate only 20 percent of the results.

The MBA and the Employability Myth

On which side of Pareto's distribution do you believe the MBA is as an effort to improve employability?

Understanding the Labor Market

It is possible that you check job listings periodically, only to verify that nothing fits you. If you are unemployed, you probably check them every day, and your conclusion may be even more hopeless: You never meet the requirements. When you find a job that could fit your qualifications, you apply, but they never call you. Maybe the problem is that many companies require an MBA as a desirable condition, and you don't have one.

If you reach conclusions about the labor market from published job offers, you probably will reach the wrong conclusions because published job offers correspond to what is called "the visible labor market." And guess what. They represent only 20 percent of the labor market, as if it were an iceberg, and you can see only the tip. Do you realize that 80 percent of job seekers compete for 20 percent of the visible job offers? Pareto's law explains it to perfection. For the remaining 80 percent of jobs, only 20 percent of candidates compete because those jobs are never published. That is the "hidden labor market."

Those who compete in the visible labor market are fighting there where there is more competition and therefore where it is more difficult to demonstrate unique value.

But that's not all. Even in the visible market, those who hold the scarcest competencies of the demanded have assured 80 percent of success. Here are some examples of scarce competencies: languages, specific strategic knowledge, international experience, management experience, and knowledge of technology. In any case, the MBA can only break a tie, as I said before. It is not the determining factor that will give you a significant advantage, and it does not qualify as a scarce quality. *Wouldn't it be wiser to spend two years in the workplace preparing yourself to win the battle than to mortgage your future to buy a tie-breaking joker?*

I interviewed some people who could share their personal experiences for this book. One of them whose opinion I value is a former student and professor at one of the most prestigious European business schools. Today he is an expert in recruitment, head hunting, placement, and career restructuring. He has many years of experience with prestigious international consulting groups. Unfortunately, he did not authorize me to publish his name. After a long discussion in which he tried to persuade me, without success, of the added value of business education, he came to the conclusion that he was not interested in relating himself to this project, and I understand. Nevertheless, he admitted what any expert on the labor market will say to you: To complete an MBA to find a better job is not the best strategy. He told me, "When a company looks for a professional, fifty percent of its search is based on the person, then on her experience. To increase employability nowadays, it is necessary to increase professional visibility. An MBA program must be done with a strategic goal, not to get a job." Check it out for yourself. Talk to people who know the labor market, not only with those who want to sell you an MBA program.

Christian Bang Rouhet, a former human resources director and human resources consultant I mentioned earlier, also affirms that today, very few companies demand an MBA as an excluding condition for a job, and if they do, it is generally for top management positions only.

The companies that demand an MBA to climb to top management positions were already scarce, and they are even more scarce today. According to an article in *The Wall Street Journal*,[89] an increasing number of companies are no longer emphasizing the diploma, and those who still do so continue to put more emphasis on professional experience. A *BusinessWeek* article[90] questions the value of the MBA degree and reveals the results of a study showing that the MBA is not a requirement for top management positions and that only 30 percent of the best-paid CEOs have an MBA. I will let you make your own conclusions. Don't you think that those brilliant professionals would have reached their current positions even if they had not done these onerous studies? That is what the author of the article suggests.

Putting Light on the Hidden Labor Market

The MBA Bubble

Besides understanding the composition of the demand of labor market, you must also understand its dynamics. Most jobs that appear in the visible market have passed through a hidden first phase in which the company tried to fill the vacancy through internal promotion and then through networking. Therefore, the key step you must take to increase your employability is to shed light on the hidden labor market.

> *"To increase your employability drastically, you must focus your efforts on seeing and being seen in the hidden labor market."*

That is the key effort that will provide more than an 80 percent probability of a satisfactory result with 20 percent of the effort. In taking that step, you will not need to spend the resources that you would dedicate to do an MBA.

If you have no idea how to shed light on the hidden labor market, ask for the help of a professional coach or a placement specialist. With their help, you can increase your chance of success. They can teach you how to master social networks to perfection, develop an intelligent networking strategy oriented to your professional project, and to sell yourself effectively in an interview. They also can help you identify your training needs. For example, it is likely that taking a course in a new technology will increase your employability more than an MBA will.

The MBA and the Employability Myth

I have tried these types of professional services and I assure you that they add much more value than an MBA.

The Holes in Your Résumé

If you are unemployed, you probably are already terrified about having a "hole" in your résumé. Having a gap in your employment history is, in general, something that worries employers. For that reason, many people think that an MBA seems to be the ideal solution to fill the hole. *Why not? It is a valuable degree that will stay on your résumé for life.*

It is indeed advisable to avoid showing periods of stagnation on your professional path, especially if the gap last for more than one year. But choosing to pursue an MBA, which will result in an enormous amount of debt with a decade payback period, is not the best solution. Instead you can train yourself strategically in scarce skills. Or you can undergo valuable (though not necessarily expensive) training abroad that will help you learn other languages; it could open doors for an international experience. Or you can launch a start-up. Or you can offer freelance services. Or you can work for free for the value of the experience. All of these solutions are infinitely more profitable that to pursue an MBA just for the sake of filling your résumé.

Richard Vacher, the senior expert in outplacement and the labour market I mentioned earlier, agrees that it is not wise to have a long period of stagnation on your résumé because it worries employers and can generate doubts about your ability to commit to a professional project. Taking one year "to live life" is generally not viewed favourably. Doing consultancy or participating in unpaid collaborations, even part-time, can complete a résumé in a positive way. According to Vacher, a master's degree is not going to increase a candidate's chance of getting a job, especially if the degree is not accompanied by professional experience.

Although Vacher admits that most of the time an MBA is well valued on a résumé, he says there are cases in which it has a negative impact. He says, *"An employer needs to have confidence about the person he or she is going to hire.* If the employer is a self-made person, a candidate with too many diplomas can be disturbing. According to the position or the environment of a job offer, sometimes it is better to remove the degree from the résumé."

The MBA as a Luxury Dinghy

A dinghy is a precarious boat with which African immigrants try to cross the Mediterranean Sea to reach Europe. They are moved by the dream of a prosperous life full of opportunities. To be able to have their seat on the small boat, they are forced to pay a fortune, which often represents their entire life savings and their family's. And their dreams are not always fulfilled.

Very often, either because of a lack of local opportunities or the desire for an international career, many applicants sign up for an MBA in a different country from that of their principal residence with the hope of finding a job abroad. They have the illusion of having bought a ticket on a small luxury dinghy.

I changed my country of residence twice and found a job both times. It is important to find a way to socialize with the locals to understand how the local labor market works. My MBA was important in that respect. But it was excessively expensive in terms of money and effort. I obtained better results with a placement service I could count on when I came to France, in spite of the fact that I hardly spoke French.

If you want to change countries, you can find an activity, training, or a professional service that will help you socialize and improve your language skills. Decide what you need and how much you can pay to get it; do not buy a Hummer if what you need is just a vehicle for going to the grocery store. Maybe a bicycle is enough. Pursue a master's degree or training only if you believe it will add something strategic to your career, and *be specific*. If you do decide to pursue a master's degree (in whatever field you choose), do not let yourself be swayed by the marketing of top institutions. Even when their prestigious brands have plenty of benefits, my experience with top schools is extremely negative in this regard. If I were to do it over, I would choose a small and promising institution that is seeking to build a name. I have come to the conclusion that smaller schools are more engaged in students' satisfaction and that they will offer more careful and personalized service. But none of them can guarantee results.

Many countries, as is the case in France, have excellent public employment services that hire private subcontractors to help people find work. You can enlist these services for free, and they will put in touch with local companies and even check your spelling when you apply for jobs. Why do you need a master's degree if you can get what you need for free?

The Career Services of Business Schools

But aren't career services departments at business schools supposed to facilitate graduates' access to the hidden labor market?

It depends. If you have the ideal profile to be employed in investment banking, venture capital work, or management consulting, it is possible that companies from those industries recruit at business schools. But hires from those sectors (which are affected by the financial crisis and have laid off too many MBAs), represent a very low percentage of total MBA hires— may be no more than 10 percent.[91] These industries are the exception to the rule, and I will talk about them at the end of the book. Let's see what happens with hires in the rest of the market.

In the case of my school, the career services department was often only one more intermediary to overcome in my effort to get an interview. Most of the available offers on its website were also published in the websites of other head-hunting companies. Anyone could apply directly, regardless of whether or not they had attended

The MBA and the Employability Myth

the business school or had an MBA degree. I did not receive any exclusive treatment based on my status as a graduate. The students had to do all of the work.

Business schools do not have any motivation to do the work that student are forced to do themselves. In fact, many students spent a lot of time at the career services office trying to flatter those in charge on the bet that they would be the recipients of some privileged, "secret" information. Couldn't they just flatter anyone who could give them some valuable information without spending a fortune in tuition?

The career services department used to organize employment fairs that attracted prestigious recruiting companies. Graduates walked by, perfumed and well dressed with a résumé and a smile, and left the decorated piece of paper at each of the tables. If you ask any labor-market specialist, they will tell you that employment fairs are a futile effort. Fairs belong to the most competitive visible market, and applicants are treated impersonally. Employment fairs at business schools can allow you to approach a big company in a more direct way, but you will have to compete with all of the other candidates who have managed to approach the same company. I do not see how the effort can be worth it. Do not forget the 80/20 rule.

You may think that the networking you can engage in via an MBA program is the key to accessing the hidden labor market. What network is more powerful and exclusive that the one you can build at a business

153

school? Isn't that the way you improve employability—by completing an MBA?

It is…if you think that you have no other alternative.

14
If You Didn't Go to Business School, You Don't Know Them

The principal disease of man is the anxious curiosity of what he cannot know.

Blaise Pascal, French Philosopher

Overrated. Overvalued. This is what I think about the network that you generate in an MBA program.

I do not mean that you are not going to meet many extraordinary and smart people in an MBA program. On the contrary, *you will meet incredible folks...like you.* You are in the MBA because of the same circumstances as the rest of the students, and they are like you. You meet people like yourself in many places: in a meeting at a friend's house, in your professional life, playing sports, going to a dance, or taking a French course. People like you are everywhere where you go.

You may think that is not the same, that an MBA program provides intensive networking with the most intelligent people who have the highest potential. In addition, when you see the price of tuition, you might think that only wealthy families can pay it, so you may reason that you will have friends from high society if you go to business school. You may think that you may never know them all in such little time if you do not get an MBA. But if you think that business school is the only place you will meet smart, wealthy, or experienced people, it may be that you are insecure and are undervaluing yourself. The truth is, at business school, you will meet people exactly like you.

Many people apply to an MBA program believing that if they are admitted, it will open the doors for them to enter an elite club. This is far from being true.

As I was growing in my professional career, the idea of an MBA as an expensive, exclusive membership seemed to be increasingly ridiculous to me because I knew many more exceptional people out of business school than in business school, as much from a personal point of view as from a professional point of view. That's simply because there are more people outside than inside business schools.

My experience has shown me that interesting people are open to speaking with other interesting people and to exchanging ideas without asking for a certificate. Do you doubt it? Do you realize that even if you do not go to business school, you will still meet intelligent, talented, wealthy people? People who can provide you with valuable information, who can teach you something, who can make you laugh while drinking a beer, or whom you could help also? Not everybody has fallen into the marketing nets of business schools. Many people have the intelligence and the qualities to be admitted but think business school is not worth it.

If You Didn't Go to Business School, You Don't Know Them

I believe that networking in business school was always overrated and that is even more so today. In the information and social networks era, to be in touch with whomever you want has never been so easy. In fact, I did a simple test. I do not have thousands of contacts on Facebook or LinkedIn. Without taking into account the contacts from my MBA—among them several professors—I verified if I could contact people from Harvard Business School. I am not American and have not lived in the United States, so that is a pretty difficult challenge. It turned out that I have some direct contacts and many second-order contacts who have studied business at Harvard. And in the same way, without taking into account the MBA network, I know people from many top business schools worldwide. I know them, I can ask them questions, and through them I can access their contacts. I also know many people without any blue-letter certificates who hold positions of responsibility all over the world. And successful entrepreneurs. People who can answer any kind of questions.

If instead of having done the MBA, I had spent two years working, I would have known so many wonderful people like those I knew at business school during that time. The only difference would be that those people would be much more related to my professional career.

Overrated.

The Myths of the MBA Network

The MBA Bubble

If you want to create an intelligent networking strategy, there is a book you must read: Keith Ferrazzi's *Never Eat Alone: And Other Secrets to Success One Relationship at a Time*.[92] In the book, Ferrazzi tells about his days at Harvard. He realized that his humble origins were an advantage for him as he faced his highly competitive classmates who, according to him, were completely wrong about how to connect with people. He wondered, "How the hell did these guys get here?"[93] His colleagues had neither the skills nor the strategic knowledge needed to connect with the others or to obtain long-term success...knowledge that, according to Ferrazzi, is not taught at business schools.

Ferrazzi affirms that it is very important to belong to the club" of the wealthy. Nevertheless, it does not mean "to share a pedigree." That does not create the links that makes people help each other. What creates links is the way in which we connect with each other.

You may have read something like this in the marketing leaflet of the business school of your choice: "The Ivegotyou Business School counts on an international network of many thousands of impressive graduates in top-responsibility positions in countless countries." Well, on LinkedIn, I can count on a much bigger network at a much lower price.

When I came to live to France and started looking for a job, I tried to capitalize on the network of business school graduates living in France. I looked for them and contacted them, and many of them answered me. *They were strangers*. I also contacted hundreds who did not

If You Didn't Go to Business School, You Don't Know Them

have an MBA, and they answered me, too—sometimes well and sometimes with distrust. It turned out that the most effective thing to do was to contact people who had a relationship with the professional path to which I was aspiring more than those who had a piece of paper with the same typography. I found the people I needed to talk with, and I connected with them. You should also be able to build such an effective network without paying a high price.

Philip Delves Broughton is emphatic on this point in an article he wrote for *The Economist*:[94] "There is no point acquiring a global network of randomly assembled business students if you just want to work in your home town. Also, they will recall that the most effective way to build a network is not to go to school, but to be successful. That way you will have all the MBA friends you could ever want."

Touché.

The truth is that you will know many amazing people in the MBA program, but you will be friends with only a few of them. You will keep in contact with them throughout your life, as with the four friends from college with whom you talk to from time to time. As for the rest, they will be open to speaking with you if you need them to, and you will follow their path on social networks…as with any person you know. Most likely, very few or even none of them will be ever related to your professional path. The rest of the impressively thousands are and will continue to be strangers, and you will have as much access to them as any other stranger has.

Do you doubt it? How would you treat someone who asked you for information about his career (which means he is looking for a job) and said he went to the same high school as you did? Probably with prudence, as you would treat any stranger. Then, before applying to the MBA program to get into an enormous network of strangers with whom you have never connected, learn to contact and to connect with the right "strangers" who are going to give you the information you need. You do not need a certificate to contact people; all you need is a strategy and a few minimal skills. Read Ferrazzi's book; it costs only $18. Play golf, subscribe to a social professional network, try to contact people you don't know. It is not complicated.

Do you want more? I offer you this excerpt from the brilliant book by Jeff Jarvis titled *What Would Google Do?*[95]

> Another byproduct of a university's society is its network—its old-boy network, as we sexistly if accurately called it. That club has long held value for getting jobs, hiring, and making connections. But now we have the greatest connection machine ever made— the Internet. Do we still need that old mechanism for connections? LinkedIn, Facebook and other services enable us to create and organize extended networks (any friend of yours...) springing out of not just school but employment, conferences, introductions, even blogs. Members of Skull and Bones at Yale and

If You Didn't Go to Business School, You Don't Know Them

graduates of Harvard Business School may object, but as an Internet populist, I celebrate the idea that old networks could be eclipsed by new meritocracies. Facebook didn't just bring elegant organization to universities; it could supplant them as a creator of networks.

Common sense, pure common sense. The exclusivity of an MBA program's networking would make more sense if the circles in which you knew people were much more closed and inaccessible. Nowadays you can access almost anyone without intermediaries.

Overrated.

But maybe you think that having shared time in classrooms with extraordinary people is not the only part of the MBA experience that will open doors for you. It is also the fact that you are receiving certification that you have been trained and that you have acquired some knowledge and skills demanded by the market. Because not everyone possesses them, the MBA may give you an advantage in your professional life.

Well, that could be true…if you think that you will access a hermetic sanctuary of wisdom that you cannot access otherwise.

15
If You Didn't Learn It in Business School, You Don't Know It

"I thought I was rich, with a flower that was unique in all the world, and all I own is an ordinary rose."

The Little Prince, Antoine de Saint-Exupery

"Mariana, she knows it all. What we have learned during the program, she knows it all through her own experience!" This was the declaration of one of my MBA classmates about the knowledge her sister had acquired by managing the family business. He was half impressed, half terrified. The way in which he said it to me made me think of the disappointment of Saint-Exupery's Little Prince when he discovered that his flower was not unique, but there were thousands of ordinary roses like his.

The truth is that his rose was quite valuable because it was his. But indeed, it was not unique.

I do not think that you will not be able to learn on your own or through professional experience what you can learn in the MBA program. We are living in the Information Age, in which knowledge is available with an amazing rapidity and at an incredibly low cost. Dale Stephens shows, in his book *Hacking Your Education*[96],

The MBA Bubble

that many people who dropped out of college could get a job and evolve in leading companies by learning on their own what they needed, even though a bachelor's degree is almost without exception a requirement to apply for a job. How couldn't you learn by yourself what you need to enhance your career? The MBA is not even a requirement and you can learn everything you need by your own.

What They Teach You in an MBA Program

What they supposedly teach you in an MBA program is all of the relevant theory you need to know about the key functions of a big established business. They supposedly train you to analyze real-life business cases so that you can make prudent decisions in a top management position.

You will supposedly also master useful skills like communication, personal productivity, and leadership that will make you stand out from the rest of your colleagues.

Why do I say "supposedly"? Because many people already question the effectiveness of MBA methods and program contents. I will not talk about that right now. Instead, I challenge you to analyze the relevancy of what they teach in an MBA program.

Everything in a business is related: finance, operations, sales, marketing, information systems, human resources, long-term strategy, etc. To understand how

If You Didn't Learn It in Business School, You Don't Know It

the different areas are interrelated and how they influence the result of the business provides an advantage when making some decisions. And an MBA teaches that.

The only "but" is that it is quite likely that you will not use this knowledge to add value for years. Also, you could acquire that knowledge on your own as you need it, which is smarter and more efficient. Remember what Napoleon Hill said in his book Think and Grow Rich: *"Knowledge will not attract money unless it is organized and intelligently directed."*[97] What sense does it make to pay a fortune to access hundreds of business cases that supposedly will teach you how to make decisions that you will not have the power to make for years, if ever? Even if learning some notion of marketing is a "nice to have" knowledge, what sense does it make to read a dozen marketing business cases about massive consumer goods product launches if you are an IT project manager? Even if you are promoted to IT director a few years later, this knowledge will be useless or obsolete. What will be the impact of business school in your career? Even if you don't know the answer, your employer does, and your salary will not change because you get an MBA

Remember that you will not be hired for a management position in which you can make that kind of decisions if you do not have the experience for it. An MBA is not going to transform you into a manager. Knowledge without practice will fade away or become obsolete. After graduation, you will use probably no more than 20 percent of what you have learned. You could have acquired that knowledge as you needed it without interrupting your professional experience.

Undoubtedly, knowing how to do effective presentations and to speak in public are valuable skills. But what use are you going to make of these skills if you are a financial analyst who never has to do presentations to anyone but your boss? In any case, thousands of effective courses are available on this topic, and you can train yourself if it is a requirement for doing your work.

But let's suppose that you are very lucky and you get to make top management decisions immediately after graduation. Even in this case, I am going to question whether an MBA program is the best place to train yourself to understand business. According to Mintzberg,[98] since 1940, business has changed rapidly, but the knowledge transmitted by elite business schools like Harvard, Stanford, or Columbia has not. In fact, the most valuable knowledge about business does not come from business schools, as pointed out by the AMLE study.[99]

Let me explain it to you using facts. In the management consulting industry, the knowledge and analysis abilities acquired in an MBA program are pertinent. To propose solutions to problems that big companies face, it is necessary to have a deep vision of all a company's functions, and the MBA provides that vision. For that reason, big management consulting groups hire people with the diploma. But not all of the hires hold an MBA. A significant percentage of the consultants come from

If You Didn't Learn It in Business School, You Don't Know It

other disciplines.[100]. Therefore, it is necessary to train them in the basic knowledge of the functioning of a big company. Do you know how long the training course is that replaces the knowledge acquired in two years of an MBA program? Three or four weeks. Ouch! A report from the Boston Consulting Group affirms that its non-MBA consultants were receiving better evaluations than their MBA colleagues. A McKinsey study reveals that non-MBA consultants were as successful as those holding the degree.[101] Ouch again! The trend of companies hiring non-MBA is growing. I am not at all surprised.

If we speak about the capacity of an MBA program to teach you how to make management decisions, I have more bad news. Henry Mintzberg is the biggest critic on the capacity of the MBA to train managers. He mentions in his book[102] a study that shows that almost two-thirds of MBA graduates use almost none of the skills that they learned in business school—or use them only marginally—in their first management positions. Isn't that supposed to be the moment when those skills would be the most useful? That's disturbing. My experience supports Mintzberg's point: *Management cannot be learned in a classroom; it should be learned by doing.* And all of the functional knowledge that is learned in an MBA program is OK, but management *is not* functional knowledge—it is *about* it. It can help, but only in the moment in which you are going to use that knowledge. Otherwise, acquiring it is a useless effort. It is like learning a language and never speaking it. You can acquire this knowledge in a much more efficient and profitable way.

The MBA Bubble

Josh Kaufman's work in his book and manifesto titled *The Personal MBA*[103] is brilliant. He selected the best business books available and put the list on his website.[104] By reading a book per week for two years in combination with professional experience, you will have exactly the same knowledge of someone with an MBA. Reading those books is a considerable effort, but it is much more efficient than the titanic financial and personal effort of completing an MBA. You do not need to read them all. You can begin with the most pertinent to your career. By the way, Kaufman's book summarizing the most important business concepts costs less than $10 in its e-book format. I cannot help thinking about the impressive ROI that this book represents. If reading alone is not exciting to you and you need a coach, Kaufman offers a training program that costs many times less than an MBA.

Josh Kaufman's *Personal MBA* is even more pertinent if you dream of launching your own business. Instead of going to business school to learn how to be a corporate servant for life in a company from the last century, you can choose to learn the twenty-first century way of doing business without burying yourself in debt. You can apply lean strategies to test your market hypothesis, and you can have a system adapted to the life you want to live. And if you find a mentor, someone who has achieved what you want to achieve, you will have the best professor in the world. This is the added value of real-life entrepreneurs' training programs. If you want to become an entrepreneur, you need to learn many concepts about business, but an MBA program is far from being the best place to do it.

If You Didn't Learn It in Business School, You Don't Know It

Diploma vs. Self-Education

You will not be able to certify what you learn on your own, whereas an MBA is a diploma you can put on your résumé. Maybe you are not skilled in learning on your own. You may need someone who encourages you to sit and study. Maybe you need structured information, presented to you. You may just need the pressure of passing an exam to learn.

It is understandable. But at least recognize that there is a difference between what the MBA teaches you and what it helps you certify. If you cannot sit down and study unless you are forced to, then you should know that what you are paying for with an MBA is an old-fashioned teacher to punish you when you do not do your homework. For much less money, a coach can give you the same results. You can also follow the ideas in Dale Stephen's book:[105] you can form a group of buddies that encourages you to be disciplined and follow your training.

If you do not have the aptitude to educate yourself constantly, you will remain behind. The world is evolving at a madman's pace, and you need to acquire new knowledge and skills on a regular basis. If you continue with the last century's paradigm that states that you will stop studying when you leave school with your diploma, you will find it very difficult to continue in the race. Fortunately you will continue learning from your experience. You cannot stop learning, and the sooner you start learning on your own, the better.

The MBA Bubble

In my opinion, diplomas will have less and less value in the future because the knowledge needed to succeed in business is increasingly specialized and practical. If you doubt it, ask specialists on the labor market. Make yourself useful to your employer by moving beyond the same general knowledge that thousands of other professionals have. I seriously wonder every day if I will incite my son to get diplomas instead of getting an intelligent self-education.

I am not the only one who thinks like this. I transcribed a few words from the Spanish writer and entrepreneur Sergio Fernandez's book *Vivir sin Miedos* (*Living Without Fear*).[106] He says this:

> In the professional or in the personal aspect, there are no secrets. You need to work yourself and what you can offer to others in order that it becomes inevitable to receive what you wish.... Forget degrees and diplomas. Ask yourself what problems you can solve for others or how you can make them earn more money or live happier. Find the answer and the rest will come.... Nobody wants to know how many courses you have attended or where you have studied, but everybody will be glad to listen to you if you explain how these courses or degrees will help them.

My experience has shown me that even employers trust "official" diplomas less than they used to. I did not take them into account when I had to hire people. I don't mean that employers do not value diplomas on a résumé. I mean that, as Fernandez says, if a person

If You Didn't Learn It in Business School, You Don't Know It

cannot demonstrate in an interview how the piece of paper is going to help the company to get concrete results, it will not be taken into account in hiring you or in defining your salary. You need to offer practical skills to improve your professional results or you are getting a degree for nothing.

Knowledge Is Increasingly Accessible

I repeat, the Industrial Age is over. It is flourishing only in Asia, not in the West, where we have been living in the Information Age for quite some time. What characterizes this age is that quality information flows freely, at an amazingly high speed and at an incredibly low cost.

Knowledge is neither the exclusive property of some illuminated few ones, nor can be contained in the restricted area of a classroom. In fact, the quantity of necessary and available information has grown so much that *there is no way you could learn everything you need to know in a classroom*. It is an inefficient form of education for the Information Age.

Jeff Jarvis explains it perfectly:

> All the world's digital knowledge is available at a search. We can connect those who want to know with those who know. We can link students to the best teachers for them (who may be fellow students). We can find experts on any topic. Textbooks need no longer be petrified on pages but can link to

information and discussion. They can be the product of collaboration, updated and corrected, answering questions and giving quizzes, even singing and dancing. There's no reason my children should be limited to the courses at one school; even now, they can get coursework online from no less than MIT and Stanford. And there's no reason that I, long out from college, shouldn't take those courses, too. [107]

In addition, you already can take those courses for free. Free platforms like edX[108], formed by prestigious universities like Harvard, Berkeley, the Massachusetts Institute of Technology, and others, allow you to take some of their classes online for free. In the same spirit, Stanford, Princeton, Rice, and several other prestigious universities created Coursera,[109] another free training platform with courses on several subjects that each last for several weeks. They offer this education not only with the altruistic goal of sharing their wisdom with the world. They do it because they realize that traditional programs are living their last days and because they are finally taking a train to the future. They offer free material as a marketing strategy to sell premium online content.[110] It is a good thing that they finally decided to redesign the future of education and of business.

If you want a closer look at business school without actually attending, you can read the books written by those who have been there, or buy for less than $10 Harvard's business cases in the online shop of the *Harvard Business Review*.[111] What you will need to know throughout your life is too specific, too

If You Didn't Learn It in Business School, You Don't Know It

perishable, and simply too vast to try to learn it in one or two intensive years. It is nonsense.

I don't deny that some professors left me open-mouthed (not all of them!), but it is always possible to attend seminars with brilliant people to have this type of learning experience. Smart people who have valuable knowledge to transmit do not exist exclusively in business schools.

Oh, the MBA learning experience! The entire MBA life-changing experience! Though many of my colleagues soon understood that it was not going to be a profitable investment, almost all of them valued the wonderful experience of spending the time of their life at business school. Almost all of them except me.

16
A Unique and Incomparable Experience...Isn't It?

Oh, the good times when we were so unhappy!

Alexander Dumas

What a wonderful experience some of my colleagues had in the MBA program! Few of them regret the experience. Maybe it was a ruinous investment for many, but it was a great experience. I am one of the few who did not enjoy it, but I am not the rule. So I guess that if you leave your job to plunge into one- or two-year MBA program, chances are that you will value the time you will spend at business school.

Before explaining why it will be a great experience for most, I will tell you why it was not a good experience for me. It was my first year of marriage, and the ninety-hour study weeks stole that family experience from me. While my husband was going to the mountains on a trek with our friends on the weekend, I stayed home preparing operations business cases. I would have preferred being with them. During that time, I felt that my life did not belong to me anymore. I realized that if that was the reality that they were training me for in my professional life, I would never have my life back.

But I was the exception. Most MBA students were single. Many of those who had a partner broke off the relationship during the program. We were spending so many hours together that it was usual to extend the day up to late hours with a few beers. Parties were frequent, and it was common for students to be hung over the following day in class. During the summer, many of my classmates went on holidays together, and they made the most wonderful memories on those trips: the fairs in Seville, the "Fallas" in Valencia, the San Fermin bullfight festival in Pamplona, skiing in the Pyrenees, or taking short trips to European capitals.

It was great to share so many hours with such extraordinarily brilliant and interesting people of the same age. Studying was exhausting, but it was also stimulating, and from that experience many groups of friends were born. They are still in touch today.

An MBA is a significant effort, but it has also generates a positive college experience. To the wonderful social experience associated with an MBA program, you can add the learning experience itself. Indeed, learning is a pleasure in itself, and the intellectual challenge of many of the classes (not all of them) was very stimulating.

Leaving aside exceptions like mine, getting an MBA is usually considered as a great experience, in spite of what they call the "W" of mood. During the program, students' self-esteem follows the way of a W: When the applicant is admitted, self-esteem is in the clouds. Then he or she starts suffering the pressure and the pace of overwhelming work. The stress and exhaustion push

A Unique and Incomparable Experience ... Isn't It?

self-esteem to the ground. Once the student graduates, self-esteem returns to its highest point. And then the graduate begins to look for a job...you can guess the rest.

Still, getting an MBA is a great experience. That is one of the reasons very few regret it even if it did not have the impact they expected in their professional career.

In fact, this is one of the biggest unconscious motivations of many of MBA applicants: to take some kind of a holiday or to go through a kind of college-days revival.

If this is what you want and you are willing to pay the price (or if someone is willing to pay it for you), that's great. But if that is what you are looking, don't lie to yourself and say that you are investing in your professional career. It is possible that the move will not turn out well.

Professional careers can stagnate soon. The day-to-day routine can turn into a boring or stressful experience. You can realize after a couple of years that you don't like your work. How do you solve that problem? By escaping to pursue an MBA and take some holidays? Wrong answer. The problem of having this motivation and not recognizing it is that you will simply postpone your dissatisfaction for several years. You will find the same type of work you had before doing the program when you graduate, and nowadays it is quite probably that you will do it at the same level of salary. And the

177

The MBA Bubble

story will start over again, only that this time you will be one or two years older and you will have to pay back a fortune for decades.

I remember some of the conversations I had with my colleagues who were trying to change my negative vision of the MBA. "Mariana, you will see when you finish the program. You will remember it as one of the best things that happened to your life," they said. But I never saw it that way. However, I admit that it is due to my personal and particular situation, and it was a wonderful experience for the rest. Nevertheless, though it has been great for many, I cannot understand why an MBA can be a better experience than other life-changing experiences that do not require you to bury yourself in debt up to your eyeballs and to study ninety hours a week.

A few months ago, a reader of my blog sent me the link to his website,[112] where he describes his adventure around the world on his motorcycle. The cost of this experience was around € 30 000 (~ $40,000) and was an accelerated education in languages, multicultural communication, and even in business. Anyone can be much more open-minded after an experience like that. Your imagination can be stimulated, and you will meet lots of amazing people who can change your life.

A colleague's husband lived through a similar experience when he was single. With a few years of professional experience, this young Dutch professional quit his job at an important petroleum company. For one year, he crossed the American continent from north

A Unique and Incomparable Experience ... Isn't It?

to south on his motorcycle. Back in Holland, he returned to knock on the door of his former employer, who received him back with open arms.

Most countries permit unpaid leave for personal projects. You can launch a start-up, travel the world, learn several languages, take part in a community mission, do nonprofit work, or have any other life-changing experience. You can always find a way to put a positive spin on such an experience on your résumé when you are in your twenties.

Why would you choose to get an MBA to spend hours with your nose immersed in hundreds of cases? Why not compare the MBA college experience with other life-changing experiences? I like to use the principle that everything must be evaluated in contrast to its alternatives. The MBA experience is no different. And because it was a negative experience for me, I cannot avoid thinking about all the fabulous experiences I might have had with less than half the money.

In conclusion: Yes, getting an MBA is an extraordinary experience. But no, it is not unique and incomparable.

Let me warn you about the danger of getting an MBA for the wrong reasons, especially if you are not conscious of them. It is too significant of a personal and financial investment to assign it to the "holiday" line of your accounting. Even if you are not the one who pays for it, getting an MBA can have consequences in your life that you must evaluate before taking the plunge.

The MBA Bubble

It is difficult to be aware of the unconscious reasons that push us to do something. If your unconscious wants something, it will push you to lie to yourself to get away with it while you think that you have been completely rational.

17
The Master of the Universe

*We shouldn't be looking for heroes;
we should be looking for good ideas.*

Avram Noam Chomsky,
American Linguist and Philosopher

When I was a child, a cartoon that was popular among the children featured a superhero who acquired amazing powers by raising his sword and shouting to the sky: "By the power of Grayskull, I have the power." After a heap of sparkles, an ordinary man and his fearful feline became He-Man and his fierce tiger...He-Man and the Masters of the Universe. Everybody in my generation knows He-Man. Every boy wanted to be like He-Man, and every girl wanted to be like She-ra, his female counterpart.

Then we grew up and became serious adults who make rational and weighted decisions.

But sometimes we continue being children inside. We continue being insecure, and we continue dreaming. We have learned to suppress our feelings, and that has made us believe we don't feel the way we did when we were children.

We are like children, although we are not conscious of it. And we continue dreaming of having a sword that gives us the automatic power to stop being simple, ordinary beings and to turn into The Master of the Universe, like He-Man.

A funny TV ad parodies car buyers. Once they leave the dealership with their new car, they start shouting like crazy like they did as children receiving a Christmas gift they were expecting. Nobody is shocked by this ad because we all know that we are like children. Car companies know it, and that's why they focus their advertising on that aspect of our humanity. Business schools also know it.

Rankings, press releases, pedigree...the whole marketing montage of business schools is specially effective when it is directed at those who feel insecure or ordinary and want to become heroes.

I am not saying that all MBA applicants are insecure. I am saying that some of them apply because they distrust their own possibilities. They hope that the degree and the pedigree will give them "the power." They don't know how it will happen, but they dream of turning into the heroes they see in the leaflets.

Richard Vacher, the outplacement expert I mentioned earlier, admits that an MBA can help increase self-assurance, although it is just a psychological effect rather than the fact that the degree contributes more professional value. Vacher tells about a man who, after

The Master of the Universe

experiencing a traumatic layoff at the age of fifty-two, pursued an MBA and recovered his self-confidence. Going back to school at that age helped him recover self-esteem. This confidence helped him get a job as general manager of a small enterprise. Nevertheless, the adventure lasted only one year because, even though he had acquired functional knowledge, it was not validated by his experience, and he did not have the necessary skills for the job.

What would this person have achieved if he had recovered his self-confidence for other means? Maybe he would have developed strategic skills that could have given him a sustainable competitive advantage in the job market. Maybe he would have aspired to jobs that were better aligned with his professional profile.

"*Le cœur a ses raisons que la raison ne connait pas.*" It means "the heart has reasons that the reason does not know." It's a wonderful phrase by the French philosopher Blaise Pascal.[113] You can save yourself a lot of bad decisions if you are conscious that you are not as rational and objective as you tell yourself you are. Daniel Goleman, in his best seller *Emotional Intelligence*,[114] describes the case of a brilliant attorney, who after having an operation to remove a cerebral tumor, lost the aptitude to associate emotion with the logic of his thoughts. His aptitude for reason was still intact. He could list the pros and cons of his options, but he couldn't assign emotion to any of them. Without emotion, he could not make any decisions.

The MBA Bubble

We decide with our emotions. If you feel insecure, you will be susceptible to choosing options that seem to improve your self-esteem. Does it mean that they are the best options? Not necessarily. It is possible that the security they seem to provide is fictitious, that their cost does not justify itself, or that the benefit does not justify negative effects.

I don't see anything wrong with buying yourself a little self-esteem. We all need it. What is sad to me is failing to realize what we are actually buying when we think we have made a rational purchasing decision.

If we were aware that we are human beings and that we have deep intimate needs like love and human connection, maybe we would deceive ourselves less. We all want respect and recognition. We all want our parents to be proud. We all want to be proud of our achievements. Don't you? It would be nice to look important through others' eyes.

An MBA is not going to turn you into a Master of the Universe. If you want to be a hero, why do you think you cannot be a hero for yourself? Try to find a good answer for this question first. The piece of paper and the pedigree will not give you the power you are missing inside.

If you need self-confidence, there are many other things you can do to improve your self-esteem. For example, you can apply to an MBA program.

The Master of the Universe

No, I am not writing these lines after an excess of tequila. You read it right. You can apply to several business schools. Some of them will not admit you because they prefer different profiles, but others will admit you with pleasure. If you are admitted to at least one, you already have the conditions to succeed. You have "the power." Remember, business schools admit only those people who already have what it takes to be successful. So why would you continue forward and spend a fortune?

If I could go back in time knowing what I know today, I would have remained with my pretty admission letter and would have put this on my résumé: "Admitted to the MBA program of the WeAreTheBest Business School." It would not have been difficult for me to explain in an interview why I didn't enter the program. "I preferred to use that time and money to develop strategic skills to impact my employers' competitive advantage." In any case, I would be glad to know that they admitted me because they thought I would experience professional success for which they could take the credit.

In the American culture there is a prevalent catastrophe that can happen to anyone, and everyone fears it: being called a "loser." If you skip the MBA, or if you don't have a degree from a top business school, someone may call you a "loser." It hurts, I know. The fact that you don't think you need an MBA to succeed is very disturbing for those who are mortgaged for decades because they thought they needed it. So if they call you a loser, it only means that they felt like losers

The MBA Bubble

themselves before they had the diploma. They would never admit that they were smart enough to be successful but too insecure to believe they could do it by themselves and that they spent a fortune to certify the talent they already had. Most people project their own fears and insecurities through others. Someone who calls you a loser is terrified of being a loser himself.

Another option to improve self-confidence is to hire a professional coach. Take your time in choosing the right coach because, unfortunately, the market is full of charlatans. A professional coach can help you gain the confidence you need for much less money than an MBA degree.

I am not going to deny it. Some prestigious brands can open doors. Philip Delves Broughton affirms in his book[115] that when he said he had a Harvard MBA, people granted him instant credibility. But he bought that credibility for an astronomic price: $175,000. Instead of spending decades working to payback the credibility a business brand can give you, you can spend less time building your own brand and your own credibility, as Steve Jobs, Michael Dell, Richard Brandson, Tim Ferriss, Josh Kaufman, and other businessmen did without an MBA. For most MBA applicants, having the self-confidence to build their own brand based on their own success would be much more profitable than following the MBA program.

On the other hand, apart from the schools Hollywood talks about, most business education brands do not have

The Master of the Universe

much value. That's the cool thing about being a top business school in a country where the movie industry is so developed—the whole world knows about the prestige of Harvard or Stanford because everybody has heard about them in a movie. And hell, they make you pay a fortune for it! They are able to attract the most brilliant professionals in the world, while the content of the program is more or less the same in different business schools all around the world. In my European school, we studied the same business cases that the MBA students study at Harvard. I also read the Black & Decker business case Broughton talks about in his book. It is not fair for the excellent European business schools, but their brands will have value only in the circle of local professionals who have considered getting an MBA. In addition, most people don't care about the diplomas you have; they will not treat you in a different way because you have the degree. In fact, many will consider you to be pretentious if you bring it up during a conversation.

Besides, a piece of paper, even if it associates you with a prestigious brand, is not going to give you any security. I have an ex-colleague with a "Master of the Universe" from one of the most prestigious European business schools based in France. As a result of the economic crisis, she was laid off, and it has been years since she could find a stable job. The piece of paper framed and hung on her wall does nothing to improve her self-esteem. It's your achievements and the way you see yourself through them what will give you the confidence you need. If you've been through a bad professional moment, maybe an assessment of your strengths[116] will be more effective than an MBA to relaunch your career.

Don't get an MBA to feel self-confident. Identify the emotional and irrational component of your decision. If you don't, you will be easy and vulnerable prey of calculated marketing campaigns disguised as objective information.

18
Is It Possible to Have an MBA and Have a Sense of Ethics?

We may pretend that we're basically moral people who make mistakes, but the whole of history proves otherwise.

Terry Hands, English Theatre and Opera Director

Yes, you can have an MBA and have a sense of ethics. In spite of the MBA, you can. But many factors make it difficult—for example, the nature of the candidates attracted by the program. Or the training method, which does not stimulate any ethical consideration of the long-term consequences of a manager's decisions.

Business schools do not train leaders. They do not train businessmen and women to create sustainable wealth for themselves and for society. They train people to be eager to earn tons of money in the shortest possible time.

Philip Delves Broughton[117] tells how one of his classmates questioned Harvard's mission statement: "We educate leaders who make a difference in the world." "I wonder why the school can't just admit that its job is teaching people to run profitable businesses. Why does it even think that leadership can be taught in business courses?" In 2009, Broughton wrote in a blog post[118] that he wondered if Harvard's mission should be rewritten: "Where to start? Well, how about this 'difference' these leaders are making in the world? Are we talking George W. Bush? Or Jeff Skilling? Or Jeff Immelt at GE? Or John Thain at Merrill Lynch? Does the difference have to be positive for the world?" Business skills you learn at business school have nothing to do with leadership.

Do you think that those who held top management positions in the tobacco industry and that concealed the results of the first reports on the harmful side effects of tobacco were leaders? I don't, but they were businessmen.

Do you believe that those who provoked the financial crisis of 2008 were leaders who made mistakes? I don't. They were businessmen with MBAs who acted with greed and a purely short-term vision.

In my opinion, except for a few honorable exceptions, those who hold business schools' top management positions are only businessmen.

Of course it is possible to be a businessman and a leader, but you do not learn how to be both in business school.

I highly recommend that you watch the documentary *Inside Job*, which analyzes the origin of the financial crisis of 2008. You will see how academicians from

Is It Possible to Have an MBA and Have a Sense of Ethics?

prestigious universities like Harvard or Columbia wrote reports on the solvency of the Icelandic financial system without any foundation, receiving juicy amounts of money. Only businessmen.

In a strategy class in which a professor was trying to explain how to assign a price to a product, he asked us what price we would put on a bottle of water sold in a supermarket. The consensus was that it would probably cost less than $1. Then he asked us what price we would put on the same bottle of water sold in a discotheque. Probably it would cost around $3. Then he asked what price we would sell the same bottle of water for in the middle of the desert to a thirsty Patricia Botín (heiress of a financial Spanish empire).

Laughing to death, we all proposed stratospheric sums to define the price we would put on the bottle, to which the professor responded: "What are you saying? The price for the bottle is to marry me!"

It was an excellent class. But there was never any consideration for the ethical and moral limits of such decisions.

Many of my classmates had no prejudice about taking part in profitable businesses that produce weapons or tobacco. They didn't ask themselves any questions about the eventual consequences of their decisions. They considered themselves (only) businessmen.

Yes, we had a subject on ethics. But it was totally disconnected from the rest of the subjects. In ethics class, we were discussing how to treat the riot of the Indians of an Amazonian tribe in an oil field, while in the rest of the subjects we continued learning how to make short-term decisions without asking too many questions.

In her book *J'ai fait HEC et je m'en excuse* (*I Went to HEC and I Am Sorry*),[119] Florence Noiville tells how her school made Muhammad Yunus, the "banker of the poor," participate in an initiative to establish the "Social Business." The author recalls her conversation with Yunus, who did not make any anti-system or anti-capitalist speeches, nor was he against companies making big profits. He only had ideas that allowed the most excluded sectors of society to benefit from the game.

Noiville was really enthusiastic, thinking that the school was finally asking itself the good questions in reacting to the disastrous consequences of the crisis. But a meeting with a finance professor disappointed her. He said this:

> You are dreaming. Nothing is going to change. They are cosmetic measures to go with the times, but the impact is minuscule. Half the students follow the classic path, and the other half have to demonstrate a great motivation: Salary in the social economy or in the sustainable development consulting is half of what they would earn in management consulting. Nothing changes. The

Is It Possible to Have an MBA and Have a Sense of Ethics?

finance that brought us here continues. Wages in investments banks increase. The authorities of financial markets continue receiving authorization demands for highly complex products. They are not catalogued as toxic yet, but it is a question of time.

Unfortunately, this is what I think that will happen with this wave of initiatives on restoring a kind of Hippocratic Oath in business schools. Nothing is going to change; they are cosmetic measures that clean the conscience of both the institutions and graduates. However, I do believe in the commitment of some of the promoters of these initiatives. But if the greed of the schools and some students does not change, nothing is going to change. Why? Because with their high prices and deceitful marketing, schools attract many impatient people, without experience, with a high level of greed who do not have any intentions of practicing ethical consideration. Some of these students get into debt up to their teeth to go out into the world to create financial earnings that are value destroying. And unfortunately I believe that we will see more examples of this in the not-very-distant future.

Is it possible to blame only the students for their greed?

Mintzberg[120] says that business schools do not create mercenaries; they only attract them. I totally agree that they attract them, but I don't completely agree that they do not create them. Business schools also attract naïve people like me, who think that an MBA will make them better professionals. They think that the high price of tuition is nothing but the consequence of the high value

The MBA Bubble

they will reach and that they will be able to contribute to the market and to society. But soon these people are confronted with reality: The market does not value what the MBA has given to them, and high salaries are available only in jobs in which they have to "sell their souls to the devil." Many end up by selling it. Broughton describes the internal fight of many MBA students, including himself, to avoid jobs that would make them miserable. Many did not win the battle. At the end of his book, he wonders, "How can I succeed financially without losing my soul?"

Mintzberg[121] admits that, pushed to the limit, people are ready to prostitute themselves. The MBA pushes many young, brilliant professionals into a limiting financial situation. Meanwhile, business schools continue raising their prices.

Yes, it is possible to have an MBA and have a sense of ethics. But business schools do not make it easy. If they applied ethical considerations to their own business, it might stop being such a profitable business. I think that there is a magic question business schools should ask themselves and that they should teach students to ask: *Am I adding value to my customers and to society, or am I only making profit?*

According to Eric Ries in his book *The Lean Startup*,[122] organizations that make profits but destroy value engage in a "success theatre," like Enron or Lehman Brothers did. This is the way I perceive business schools: a theatre that teaches the art of performance to its students.

19
The Exceptions to the Rule

There are neither laws nor traditions nor rules that could be applied universally, including this one.

Anonymous

I know that I have spent many hours telling you why getting an MBA is a bad idea. But it is not always like that; there are exceptions. There are situations in which the degree can be a career or business accelerator. I estimate that 80 percent of those who do an MBA will not realize any differential benefit for having done it, but the remaining 20 percent will.

Let's analyze the 20 percent of the situations in which I do believe that getting an MBA is a good idea.

If my warning about working as a slave did not scare you and you love the eighty-hour-work-week lifestyle, then you will probably be interested in this. You will not have any problem working in management consulting or investment banking. In these sectors, an MBA can help you a lot. Nevertheless, if you do not have experience or connections on your résumé in financial services or consulting, trusting that the MBA will catapult you toward a career in these sectors *is a great risk*. But if you do have the experience and

195

connections, chances are that an MBA from a top school can turn out to enhance salary and employability. In these sectors, an MBA is not only highly expected; it can be a requirement. However, as I mentioned before, there is a considerable percentage of hires who do not hold an MBA, and not having it does not seem to have any impact on these professionals' results.

But in general terms, having an MBA can be a career accelerator because the knowledge and the "training" you get with an MBA are more than pertinent.

According to Henry Mintzberg,[123] the case method is pernicious for training managers because it forces them to make decisions in an industry they don't know about after reading a dozen sheets of paper. The worst part is that this stimulates the arrogance in them because they may believe they can make right decisions with such a superficial analysis.

But that is exactly what management consultants do— they analyze business situations in the least possible time, making conclusions from an industry they hardly know from an aseptic point of view, proposing solutions that the manager must validate. MBAs are trained to do this (and they are trained to work like hell, too!). If you have already started a career in consulting, you do not mind to continue working at a frenetic pace for many years and you want to boost your career, chances are that getting an MBA makes all the sense in the world. But do not forget to evaluate the profitability of your investment. I do not believe it is reasonable to

The Exceptions to the Rule

"buy" some benefits, regardless of the price. The cost of tuition has reached such stratospheric levels that maybe it is not even a good idea in this case.

The same reasoning is applied to the financial sectors. An MBA will contribute elements to help you understand how the economic activity of a company affects the value of its financial assets. It is evident that employers in the financial sector will value this kind of education if it is coherent with a career in finance. And again, if you do not have the contacts or the experience that they require of people who work in this sector, an MBA can be risky.

The reason an MBA from a top school opens doors in these sectors is the elitism and the inbreeding with which hires are made.[124] An MBA is an effective introduction letter. But be careful—you must already belong to the "elite" before getting the MBA; don't believe that a piece of paper will make you a member if you were not part of the "group" before. Getting into debt up to the teeth and believing that you will buy yourself a nobility title is a big mistake.

Remember the good skepticism. Speak with people who are in these sectors and ask for their opinions. Enlarge your network. Do not rely on the MBA as your only launch platform. Begin with intelligent networking. It is too important an investment to take it carelessly.

If you are a manager in an industrial company, congratulations. You know more about management than any recent MBA graduate, even one from a top business school. Here, again, I am with Mintzberg: Management cannot be taught in a classroom; it is something that is learned by doing. It is even possible that you have some MBAs working for you. If you are also passionate, have a need for great responsibility and power, and dream of climbing the corporate ladder, an MBA could be an accelerator.

You could consider getting an "Executive" MBA part time. How can it accelerate your career? It can help you understand better the various functional departments of your company and how the decisions in the different areas influence business, thus reducing your rate of "technical mistakes." If you had done the program at the beginning of your career, it would have been useless. But to pursue it in the moment you have to make management decisions in a sector you know deeply can provide useful tools. Nevertheless, do not expect that your company will recognize the piece of paper or increase your salary (well, you can always try). What your company will value is the increase of skills that you translate into more effective results. But if you find it easy to learn by yourself, reading books or understanding how your company works in an intuitive way, it is possible that the investment in an MBA degree is not worth it. It is also possible that avoiding expensive business schools and enrolling in a smaller one will serve your needs.

If you work for a big traditional industrial company, an MBA can be an internal requirement to be promoted to top management positions. These companies are not the

The Exceptions to the Rule

majority, but they still exist. However, even in these companies, this requirement is not always unavoidable. Sylvie Laÿs, a human resources consultant, confirmed through many of her recruitment missions that points of view differ in big corporations among departments. According to Laÿs, there is a difference between the perception of managers, who tend to value the professional experience, and that of the human resources department, which tends to favor diplomas. So if a search is initiated by the functional manager who has the need to fill a position, an MBA can have less weight than if it starts in the human resources department. For that reason, having good political skills and a connection with the potential manager will be more important than a diploma. But I am not going to deny it—in this type of organization (there are not many), an MBA can open doors to top management positions. But it will not open them all!

The MBA path might be right for you if you already have a career in an organization of this type, you already know that management is what you want for your future career, and you see clear long-term development possibilities in that company. But if that is not the case, the MBA will not give you what you do not have.

Another exception to my admonition that an MBA is not worth the time, effort, or money is when your company offers to pay for the program, on the condition that the effort required does not overwhelm you since you are probably going to double your work load while you are enrolled in the program. But if it is a fair enough deal for you, why wouldn't you accept it? If your manager is offering it to you, it is because he or she sees that it will be profitable for the company and believes in your potential. But do not expect a raise for several years. That money will go toward your degree.

What you can lose in this case is little freedom because the company may ask you to remain employed there for a certain number of years, and if you should leave the company, they may ask you to reimburse them for the cost of the program. In any case, if you find another career opportunity, your new employer might pay the amount specified in your "exit clause." This happened to an Argentine ex-colleague. His company paid for his MBA at the prestigious IMD of Switzerland, including all of the expenses for him and his family during the program. Some time later, he found out about a career opportunity through his MBA contacts. A pharmaceutical company offered him a marketing management position and paid his "exit clause." I guess that they came to the conclusion that if another company had invested so much money in him, he should be a sure value. Today, a few years later, he has a management position in the London headquarters. Completing the degree was a great idea for him.

But just in case I did not repeat it enough in this book: Do not believe that an MBA will bring you the same success it brought him. He already had demonstrated his aptitude, and the MBA degree was the consequence of his potential, effort, and talent—not the cause. When I asked him how much he valued it, he told me that it had not added as much value as his previous experience. But if the company wanted to invest in his training, why would he reject it?

An MBA is completely useless for people with little or no professional experience, but there are two cases in which I think it could be a good idea, even in that situation.

The first situation is if you are the inexperienced heir of an industrial company. You know that your future as the successor is assured, and you need to train yourself quickly to strengthen your company's long-term survival probability. The MBA program can accelerate your understanding of factors that will concern your future management of the business. It can help you discuss with your family members, who are the top managers, decisions you would make in various circumstances. In that way, you would apply in an immediate and practical way what you have learned in the MBA program. It would be an excellent way to ensure the professionalism of the future management generations of the company. But an MBA will not guarantee your success or ensure that you make the right decisions. If you do not strive to be an excellent manager for your company and don't engage in constant training, you will squander your family's fortune even if you have a top "Master of the Universe" degree.

There is another situation in which an MBA contributes value to inexperienced people, and if you are in this situation, I am really sorry for you. If you have graduated with a bachelor's degree and are affected by the lack of opportunities in the job market, your professional experience may be limited to a couple of internships, often unpaid, in which you got tired of making photocopies. I wouldn't recommend asking for another student loan to pursue an MBA because it could take decades to pay all of the money back. But if you think you do not have another way to gain valuable market experience (Are you sure you do not have another way?) and your parents offer to pay for your MBA because they love you, it might be a good idea. The fact is that if you are competing with thousands of other young professionals with the same inexperience as you, perhaps an MBA can break a tie in your favor. Some head hunters may look for credentials and potential when there is a lack of experience. But you should be aware that you will always lose the battle against someone who demonstrates interesting work experience and good results. And if you do get a job, do not trust that the MBA will open other doors for you; you will have to work hard to earn your place in the marketplace.

In the same way as I believe it is ridiculous to get an MBA to become a manager, I believe it is ridiculous to get an MBA to become an entrepreneur. But in the same way in which I believe an MBA can add value to someone who is already a manager to accelerate his or her career, I also think it can add value to someone who already owns a company of at least medium size to accelerate its growth. If your company is very small or if you are a sole proprietor, I recommend that you devote yourself to self-education with the Josh Kaufman reading list of business books I mentioned earlier or with the courses given by real-life entrepreneurs from your industry.

If your company is large, promotes itself through traditional marketing techniques, and has high growth potential, perhaps an MBA can provide some knowledge to help you manage its growth. Remember the case of my colleague, who had his own successful business and decided to follow an MBA program. I believe that it has been an excellent investment in his case (especially because he managed to negotiate a substantial tuition discount).

None of those situations applied to me or to most of my classmates. In general, I estimate that it is not the case of around 80 percent of the people who apply to an MBA program. If you are not in any of these circumstances either, please hesitate before enrolling. Analyze your decision deeply before taking such an irreversible and costly plunge.

20
My Story

"Good judgment comes from experience, and experience comes from bad judgment."

Rita Mae Brown, American Writer

Looking backward with the perspective of my experience, it is easy to me to identify the mistakes I made. But I also know that with the resources I had at that moment, it would have been difficult for me to avoid making them.

This book is not about me but about you and how you can avoid making the same mistakes I made. But to help you better understand the context of my opinions, let me tell you my story.

I was born in the suburbs of the beautiful city of Buenos Aires, the capital of Argentina, in the bosom of a well-to-do middle-class family. The value of education was something that was emphasized at home. My mother was a teacher and a successful self-made businesswoman. She managed to create several companies in diverse sectors and to amass a small fortune that gave her the freedom to acquire assets and travel the world. Her lateral thinking influenced me in a determinant way. My father was a vocational journalist.

His life was disorganized, like that of an artist. He worked an erratic schedule, and if something excited him, he could work nonstop for hours until he finished it. He always had enough work, though his independent character may have prevented him from being more successful. My parents separated when I was six years old.

It wasn't until I was an adult that I became aware that neither of them had a university degree. They were great readers and trained themselves constantly. I inherited from them a love of reading and absorbing new ideas. I always assumed I would go to college. It seemed to me that it was what I needed to do according to my family values. I studied industrial engineering at Universidad del Salvador in Buenos Aires and graduated with high grades. These studies opened the door for me to work at big, leading, multinational corporations like Telefonica of Argentina (a subsidiary of Telefonica de España, the Spanish telecommunications giant), Pluspetrol, Shell, Leroy Merlin (Home Depot's European equivalent), Saint Gobain (a French giant of building materials), and ResMed (a world leader in sleep and respiratory medicine). Although I am deeply grateful for what I learned from these experiences, I also saw that the quality of life that I might have working for big corporations was much worse than the one my parents could allow themselves. The alienation, the lack of satisfaction and freedom, the endless working hours including weekends and innumerable business trips, the lack of work–life balance, the dictatorial culture, and the politics reduced my energy and my interest for

My Story

work. Salary was my main motivation to work. I have been lucky to have bosses I admired and with whom I have a nice relationship. I always worked on stimulating projects. My results were, in general, well evaluated. And I always showed initiative. But my level of dissatisfaction did not seem sustainable to me.

At the university, I met the man who is now my husband and the father of my son. At the end of 2001, a financial crisis that the Argentinians called "the crisis of the corral" began. Then the company at which my husband was employed decided it was time to leave the country and asked him to move to Spain. It was a French multinational that had led him to live in France and Brazil a few years before. I had a great job with a high salary, a company car, and many benefits. But I was also very attracted by an international experience, and Argentina's economic future was uncertain, so we decided to accept the offer. Because I did not have a lot of time, I started to look quickly for the alternatives that would allow me to optimize the possibilities of inserting myself into the Spanish labor market. Pursuing an MBA looked like the best option. I decided to finance the degree with some savings and some help from my family so that I could avoid getting a bank loan.

It was decided. With the help of a colleague who had just gotten an MBA degree from Harvard financed by his company, I chose the school I wanted to apply to, participated in the whole admission theatre, and was admitted. I am deeply grateful for my colleague's help. He is a great person, brilliant and engaged.

Unfortunately, his sincere and well-meaning vision did not serve me in realizing that pursuing an MBA would be a mistake for me.

One of the things that worried me was whether or not I would be able to balance my studying time and my spare time because it was my first year of marriage, and I did not want to lose that personal experience. My colleague assured me that I should not worry, that achieving balance was possible. His first son was born while he was enrolled in the program, and it seemed to be perfectly compatible to him. Philip Delves Broughton also affirms in his book[125] that he never felt overwhelmed by the work load, in spite of being a person dependent on good rest. The author, married with a son, had his second son while he was getting the master's degree. I came to the conclusion that, in spite of the fact that Harvard's program must be very demanding, the work load must be more distributed throughout the two years than mine was because undoubtedly, in the master's program I did, no kind of balance seemed possible to me. The few enrolees who were married were separated from their spouses throughout much of the program.

The first weeks of the program were pure adrenaline and excitement. Everything I was learning was really exciting. Many of the professors were brilliant, and my classmates were very nice people. But little by little, I was discovering that I had certain expectations with regard to the program that would not be fulfilled, and soon I decreed that I had made a monumental mistake.

My Story

First disappointment: My business school would not help me find a job in Spain, as I expected. In spite of the fact that I had some preferent conditions to obtain a work visa because my husband was a resident of Spain, the director of career services declared that I would not get a job in Spain. According to him, if I wanted to get a job, I would have to go back to my country. Full stop. The difficulty of having to go through the procedures to get a work visa was rendering me, in his words, "unemployable." Case closed.

Second disappointment: Not only was the school turning its back on me; I also began to verify the perverse system we were feeding. I had turned into one powerless piece of someone else's "money" machine. I was earning neither freedom nor quality of life nor market value nor employability nor rare skills. I had spent my money and a lot of time so that the machine continued working for them without any guarantee that it would work for me. In a low voice, many of my classmates admitted it: Nobody would speak badly about the program officially because doing so is against one's own interests. It is a perverse business in which the customer has no power. I deeply regretted the decision I had made (and the perspective I have gained through the years has not changed that). But I did not have any other alternative than to continue running inside the wheel as fast as possible as an obedient rat until I got my diploma, or I would have thrown away all of my money.

Third and most outrageous disappointment: Without the most minimal intention of pretending, those in career services started admitting in a loud voice that the program would not have any value in the labor market in the short term. They said we should accept whatever job offers we got. "The return on investment is seen in the long term." What? What is seen in the long term is the fruit of one's personal effort!

My expectations about the master's degree were nothing more than to get some help finding a job in Spain as a product manager, the job I had in Argentina. I already knew that the market did not perceive MBA graduates as the "Masters of the Universe" that many of them think they are. But I was not prepared at all for the market to ignore my degree and for my business school to ignore me as a customer.

The program ended, I received my diploma, and I felt completely lost and without resources—like an idiot. I had spent too much time sequestered among hundreds of business cases. Faced with the business school's indifference, I did not know where to begin.

As much as I hated to admit it, I knew that the only contact I had with the "exterior world" was the business school. I began to go there every day to speak with some of the professors I have had good relationship with, being careful not to reveal how I was feeling. Finally I realized that some professors had a research budget assigned and had some vacancies for paid scholarships. The remuneration was considered to be financial aid, not a job. I would not need a work visa. That was how I obtained an invitation letter from a professor to receive a scholarship.

My Story

Among the scholars of the business school were several MBAs with or without work visas, and nobody seemed to feel sorry for them. There were also people who had graduated with bachelor's degrees from various schools, so one could accede to those scholarships without having studied at business school. But the tasks we were doing were far from being those of a "Master of the Universe."

In spite of the adamant position of the director of the career services office, I knew that finding a job would have to be possible. I had already been employed at multinational companies that were open to hiring people with multicultural profiles and were accustomed to managing work visas for them. I just had to find my opportunity. I had a couple of interviews that did not prosper, but the fact that I had interviews (which I obtained with my own effort) was a good sign.

One day a professor asked me if I had experience as a product manager. She said her husband's company was experiencing difficulty finding product managers with the profile they needed. She wondered if I was interested in going for an interview. Of course I was interested! It turned out that I had the profile they needed, and they hired me. In spite of the fact that the salary was not great, it was exactly what I was looking for: a job like the one I had had in my country. I got it one year after getting my degree. When he found out about it, the director of the career services department called me immediately and asked me how I did it. "Ah, you did it through the school," he said, and the conversation did not last much longer. He had scored.

Yes, I did it through the school. And I also did it in spite of the school. In spite of the fact that they tried to convince me that I would not do it. In spite of the fact that they turned their back on me. In spite of the fact that I had lost two years of my career doing something that was not valued by the market. In spite of the fact that I would have done it anyway if I had gotten a scholarship in a place where I could speak to people in contact with the market instead of selling my soul to the devil.

His opinion was that I did it through the school. I believe that I did it by being in touch with a person with goodwill who shared interesting information with me (and to which I am personally deeply grateful). But if I had been in contact with people in any area other than the business school, I would have had access to the same types of information, and I would have taken advantage of the same type of opportunities. It happened to me when I moved to France a few years later. It is even possible that I could have negotiated a better salary if I had not been demoralized in such a way. *When you are in trouble, they turn their back on you, and when you are successful, they take the credit.* This was exactly my experience.

This job I got "through the school" (in which I earned less than in my previous job) was one of the jobs I enjoyed most in my professional career. I worked for a French multinational retail company. I was lucky to be an *"intrapreneur"* and to rely on the confidence of a boss I admired (and who did not have an MBA degree). I built a nice friendship with her that is ongoing.

My Story

Then I followed my entrepreneurial instinct and left to join another French multinational corporation to build a new retail concept. In this experience, I could hire my own team and design my department's entire strategy. But we were surprised by the crisis of 2008, and after a little more than two years, the subsidiary decided to close the business. Then I followed my husband again, who had a new professional challenge in France, where I could count on an outplacement service. In spite of the crisis and of not being fluent in French, I managed to get a job in a different sector, the medical industry, in much less time and with much more effectiveness that I did with my MBA.

After being employed in the medical sector as a product manager for almost three years, I decided to separate from the corporate world and to redirect my career in a direction that would have made me happy from the beginning: to follow the legacy of my parents as an entrepreneur. Today I am investing in my own business, teaching and helping people with their businesses and careers. I do not blame the business school for my difficulties to get a job when I came to Spain. I do not blame it for the salary that I had after graduation either. But I do not give them the credit for the things that did go out well for me neither. Of course I am deeply grateful with certain people, but I attribute it neither to the school nor to the program, and I consider I got a very poor value for money.

As for using my MBA skills and knowledge after finishing the program, I don't think I have used more than 30 percent of what I learned in the MBA program in my career. If I had remained in the labor market during that time, I would have acquired many of them anyway. I am not going to deny it: Some classes astonished me. But because I am an avid reader, I have to say that those classes didn't surprise me more than certain powerful books that taught me valuable things and even changed my life. If I had not gone to business school, I would not have missed any knowledge from a practical point of view. That is to say, probably I would know less about finance or operations. But I never really needed this knowledge, and I would have acquired the rest in a practical way. I did not learn anything that has revolutionized the way in which I did my work. I am only grateful for the overall view of the functions of a business, but I would also have learned that by reading.

Maybe my opinion is limited to my own experience at a certain school. Nevertheless, after reading what others have written on the topic in different parts of the world about different schools, I believe I would have formed exactly the same opinion regardless of which school I attended. Surely Harvard is more prestigious than my school. But I do not see what Harvard would have given to me that was different than what I got if, to follow Harvard's program, I would have to go through a much more demanding admission process, to have three times better recommendations, and to have paid three times more money. I continue thinking that it would not have added anything to my success that I did not have before going there or that justifies its cost. Although the experience might have been different in one or another aspect, the system is the same in all of

My Story

the business schools: Students are the pieces that make the machinery work, but this machinery neither belongs to them nor benefits them.

You can see that I do not love the business-school industry like some journalists or professors do. But I do not claim that you should hate business schools. My only hope is to try to keep you from making a decision you will regret like I did.

If you do not share my values, or if you are pretty certain than an MBA will add great value to your career, do not hesitate to enroll. My goal was not to convince you of the opposite but to invite you to consider it deeply. If your enthusiasm about an MBA degree survived this book, then go for it! On the other hand, if I made you hesitate, try to go deeper, and clarify all your doubts. It is what I would have wanted—to have analyzed my decision more thoroughly.

Although I am pretty sure that I would have obtained my professional goals without the MBA, I cannot know for sure if I would have. But do not believe everything business schools say. They want your money, and it's a lot of money! The good skepticism is the one that will help you choose the right path. If I have helped you make a more informed decision to pursue an MBA, please send an e-mail to me to tell me so. If you always thought that you should have done an MBA and you got rid of all your regrets by reading this book, tell me that also. If you think that everything I say in this book is blasphemous, also send me an e-mail. I will be delighted to hear from you.

Where All This Began

When I decided to leave the corporate world, I gave myself the license to speak, finally, freely, about my opinion of the MBA. Then I wrote an article in French[126] in which I exposed many of the ideas I express in this book. It was published in one of the most-read blogs of France, "Des Livres pour changer de vie," thanks to the support of its author, Olivier Roland, an entrepreneur whom I admire. The success and the repercussions that resulted from that article made me see that I needed to take this message to more people. That is how the idea of writing this book was born.

Others have been criticized for writing books that question the value contributed by business schools, and I cannot expect less. Philip Delves Broughton was accused of writing his books about Harvard only to earn notoriety. Kaufman was criticized also because his book is the preamble of the program that he offered as alternative training to the MBA. In spite of his love for the business-school industry, Juanma Roca was also criticized for revealing a few truths about the industry. I presume that those who have interests in business schools will attack me, too. It is logical.

After reading Mintzberg's and Kaufman's books, I do not doubt their strong opinions about the MBA degree. I think they have been brave in denouncing the

My Story

perversion of a system that benefits neither society nor students. They were the most qualified to create a solution to the problem they had identified. I applaud them.

I know that this book is negative publicity for business schools. Nevertheless, let me clarify that I have no commercial interest with any of the people or solutions I present as an alternative to the MBA. If I recommend something to you, it is because I believe it can be useful.

I assure you, I have written and rewritten every word and every idea in this book in my head for the past ten years. During all of that time, I could not stop feeling the urgency to say what I was thinking because I do not want anyone to make the same mistake I made.

Acknowledgments

This book might never have seen the light of day without the unconditional support of my family and of many friends who gave me their time and attention to exchange ideas about the information I affirm. To all of them, my deep gratitude.

I would not dare to have written this book without the support of Olivier Roland, a young and successful French entrepreneur who allowed me to tap into the notoriety of his blog to transmit this message for the first time. Like all those I admire, Olivier is an open and accessible person in spite of his success. His constant orientation to add value to his customers and his common sense are just two reasons I admire him so much. His success story is the antithesis of the one of those who seek success by getting an MBA. At less than thirty years old and without any diplomas, Olivier shared with his readers the challenge of doing a "personal MBA" in one year[127]. Today, a few years later, he is one of the most educated and successful people I know.

Also I am indebted to all the people who agreed to be interviewed for this book. They have shared their know-how generously and openly.

I might never have put all of these ideas in order without the contribution of all the authors of books and articles I mention in this book. I deeply thank all of them for having dedicated so many hours of their lives to transmit their knowledge and ideas. How much less light would there be in this world if they had not decided to say out loud what they were thinking.

www.thembabubble.com

Notes

[1] Sir Ken Robinson, "RSA Animate—Changing Education Paradigms," YouTube, accessed May 13, 2013, http://www.youtube.com/watch?v=zDZFcDGpL4U.

[2] "Are MBAs Worthless?" NBC Chicago, January 22, 2013, http://www.nbcchicago.com/blogs/inc-well/Are-MBAs-Worthless-187154241.html.

[3] Raimón Samsó, *El Código del Dinero* (*The Money Code*) (2009).

[4] Philip Delves Broughton, "The Incredible Shrinking Career," *The Economist*, December 18, 2012, http://www.economist.com/whichmba/incredible-shrinking-career.

[5] "Opportunity in Adversity," *The Economist*, September 30, 2009, http://www.economist.com/node/14537489.

[6] "The End of Business Schools? Less Success than Meets the Eye," Academy of Management and Learning Education, September 2002, http://www.aomonline.org/Publications/Articles/BSchools.asp.

[7] "Is the MBA Overrated?" *BusinessWeek*, March 19, 2006, http://www.businessweek.com/stories/2006-03-19/is-the-mba-overrated.

[8] Ibid.

[9] "Ya tengo el MBA. Y ahora, quién tiene una oferta a la altura?" ("I already have the MBA degree. Who has a job offer at the height of it?") Cincodias, March 3, 2012,

http://cincodias.com/cincodias/2012/03/03/economia/13
30755660_850215.html
[10] "The End of Business Schools? Less Success than Meets the Eye," ibid.
[11] "The Great College Hoax," *Forbes*, January 14, 2009, http://www.forbes.com/forbes/2009/0202/060.html.
[12] "MBA: Think Carefully Before Taking the Plunge," June 2, 2005, http://mbacaveatemptor.blogspot.fr/2005/06/wharton-grads-caveat-emptor-for.html.
[13] Josh Kaufman, *The Personal MBA: A World-Class Business Education in a Single Volume*, 2010.
[14] "Cost of MBA Teaches Tough Financial Lesson," *Chicago Tribune*, May 18, 2012, http://articles.chicagotribune.com/2012-05-18/features/sc-cons-0517-marksjarvis-20120518_1_mba-programs-harvard-mba-student-loans.
[15] D. Soriano, "IESE: 'No Necesitas ni un Euro para Estudiar Nuestro MBA, sólo la Carta de Admisión," *Libre Mercado*, April 16, 2011, http://www.libremercado.com/2011-04-16/iese-no-necesitas-ni-un-euro-para-estudiar-nuestro-mba-solo-la-carta-de-admision-1276420671/.
[16] Philip Delves Broughton, *Ahead of the Curve* (The title outside the US is *What They Teach You at Harvard Business School*), 2008.
[17] "Think Twice," *The Economist*, January 2011, http://www.economist.com/whichmba/think-twice.
[18] "For Newly Minted MBAs, a Smaller Paycheck Awaits," *The Wall Street Journal*, January 6, 2013,

Notes

http://online.wsj.com/article/SB10001424127887324296604578175764143141622.html.

[19] "Jobless MBAs Opt for Entrepreneurship," *BusinessWeek*, June 18, 2009, http://www.businessweek.com/bschools/content/jun2009/bs20090618_346720.htm.

[20] "Ne Vous Trompez Pas: Pourquoi un MBA n'est Pas Rentable," Des Livres Pour Changer De Vie, http://www.des-livres-pour-changer-de-vie.fr/mba/.

[21] Seth Godin, *All Marketers Are Liars* (2005).

[22] Florence Noiville, *J'ai fait HEC et je m'en excuse* (*I Went to HEC and I Am Sorry*) (2009).

[23] Michael Ryall, "The MBA Tuition Bubble," May 2, 2011, http://blogs.hbr.org/cs/2011/05/the_business_school_tuition_bubble.html.

[24] Henry Mintzberg, *Managers, Not MBAs* (2004).

[25] John Byrne, "The Arguments Against Business Schools," Poets & Quants, http://poetsandquantsforexecs.com/2011/02/27/201/.

[26] Guru Huky, "Por Qué No Deberías Estudiar un MBA," (Why you shouldn't pursue an MBA) GurusBlog, October 24, 2010, http://www.gurusblog.com/archives/mba-estudiar/24/10/2010/.

[27] "MBA: Think Carefully Before Taking the Plunge," Ibid.

[28] "Is the MBA Overrated?" ibid.

[29] Beth Braccio Hering, *When having an MBA is important*, CareerBuilder.com, June 9, 2010 http://edition.cnn.com/2010/LIVING/worklife/06/09/cb.when.mba.important/index.html

[30] "Estudiar en el Exterior, un Privilegio de Pocos?" ("To Study Abroad, a Privilege for a Few?"), *La Nación*, June 16, 2011, http://www.lanacion.com.ar/1380194-estudiar-en-el-exterior-un-privilegio-de-pocos.
[31] "Llegan los MBAs de Tercera Generación" ("The Third-Generation MBAs Arrive"), *CincoDías*, September 14, 2012, http://www.cincodias.com/articulo/especiales/llegan-mba-tercera-generacion/20120914cdsesp_2/.
[32] Philip Delves Broughton, *Ahead of the curve*, ibid.
[33] Henry Mintzberg, *Managers, Not MBAs*, ibid.
[34] "El Diablo está en los Rankings" ("The Devil Is in the Rankings"), *El País*, December Mike, 2010 http://elpais.com/diario/2010/12/12/negocio/1292165247_850215.html.
[35] Juanma Roca, *MBAs, ¿Angeles o Demonios?* (2009).
[36] Ibid.
[37] "MBA: Think Carefully Before Taking the Plunge," ibid.
[38] Adam Palin, "Methodology," *Financial Times*, January 28, 2013, http://www.ft.com/intl/cms/s/2/03bd60fe-609b-11e2-a31a-00144feab49a.html#axzz2PVDzqwkx.
[39] "MBA Pay: The Devil Is in the Details," *BusinessWeek*, November 19, 2012, http://www.businessweek.com/articles/2012-11-19/mba-pay-the-devils-in-the-details.
[40] Juanma Roca, ibid.
41 "The End of Business Schools? Less Success than Meets the Eye," ibid.
[42] Ibid.

Notes

[43] "What's Wrong with MBA Ranking Surveys? Official MBA Guide," 1993, http://officialmbaguide.org/whatswrong.php.
[44] Henry Mintzberg, *Managers, not MBAs*, ibid.
[45] "The End of Business Schools? Less Success than Meets the Eye," ibid.
[46] Philip Delves Broughton, *Ahead of the Curve*, ibid.
[47] *Inside Job*, documentary produced by Charles H. Ferguson, 2010.
[48] Maria Álava Reyes, *Trabajar sin Sufrir (Working Without Suffering)*, 2008.
[49] Philip Delves Broughton, *Ahead of the Curve*, ibid.
[50] Florence Noiville, ibid.
[51] Ken Robinson says schools kill creativity, TED, accessed on May 30, 2013
http://www.ted.com/talks/ken_robinson_says_schools_kill_creativity.html
Ken Robinson: How to escape education's death valley, TED, accessed on May 30, 2013
http://www.ted.com/talks/ken_robinson_how_to_escape_education_s_death_valley.html
Ken Robinson: Bring on the learning revolution! TED, accessed on May 30, 2013
http://www.ted.com/talks/sir_ken_robinson_bring_on_the_revolution.html
[52] Robert T. Kiyosaki and Sharon L. Lechter. *Rich Dad, Poor Dad* (2005).
[53] "Is the MBA Overrated?" ibid.
[54] The MBA Is Equivalent to What Is Called HEC in France, "Les diplômes des patrons du CAC 40", Le Journal du net, accessed on May 30, 2013

http://www.journaldunet.com/management/0601/060118patrons-diplomes.shtml.

[55] Alejandro Suárez Ocaña, "El Emprendedor Que Se Engañaba a Sí Mismo" ("The Entrepreneur Who Lied to Himself"), "Hay un Gurú en Mi Sopa, diario El Mundo" blog, June 2012, http://www.elmundo.es/blogs/elmundo/hay-un-guru-en-mi-sopa/2012/06/12/el-emprendedor-que-se-enganaba-a-si.html.

[56] Philip Delves Broughton, *Ahead of the Curve*, ibid.

[57] Henry Mintzberg, ibid.

[58] Ibid.

[59] Juanma Roca, ibid.

[60] "Jobless MBAs Opt for Entrepreneurship," ibid.

[61] Napoleon Hill, *Think and Grow Rich* (1937).

[62] Josh Kaufman, *The Personal MBA: A World-Class Business Education in a Single Volume*, ibid.

[63] Josh Kaufman, "The Ninety-Nine Best Business Books," accessed on May 19, 2013, http://personalmba.com/best-business-books/.

[64] Michel Ellsberg, *The Education of Millonaires: Everything You Don't Learn in College About How to Be Successful*, 2012

[65] Robert T. Kiyosaki and Sharon L. Lechter, ibid.

[66] Ken Robinson says schools kill creativity, TED http://www.ted.com/talks/ken_robinson_says_schools_kill_creativity.html

[67] "How to Create Your Own Real-World MBA," Four-Hour Work Week blog, accessed on May 30, 2013 http://www.fourhourworkweek.com/blog/2010/06/28/mba/.

Notes

[68] "Picking Warren Buffet's Brain: Notes from a Novice," Four-Hour Work Week blog, accessed on May 30, 2013 http://www.fourhourworkweek.com/blog/2008/06/11/061108-picking-warren-buffetts-brain-notes-from-a-novice/.

[69] "Un MBA No Asegura el Éxito—El Papelito Ya no Habla," CNN Expansión, accessed on May 30, 2013 http://www.cnnexpansion.com/expansion/2010/12/17/el-papelito-ya-no-habla.

[70] "Un MBA No Asegura el Éxito—A Veces No es ni Superior ni Educación," CNN Expansión, accessed on May 30, 2013 http://www.cnnexpansion.com/expansion/2010/12/17/a-veces-no-es-ni-superior-ni-educacion

[71] Henry Mintzberg, ibid.

[72] Tim Ferriss, *The Four-Hour Work Week*, 2007.

[73] Josh Kaufman, *The Personal MBA: A World-Class Business Education in a Single Volume*, ibid.

[74] Josh Kaufman, "The Personal MBA Manifesto," accessed May 19, 2013, http://personalmba.com/manifesto/.

[75] Seth Godin, "Good News and Bad News," Seth Godin's blog, March 2005, accessed on May 30, 2013 http://sethgodin.typepad.com/seths_blog/2005/03/good_news_and_b.html.

[76] Godin, Seth, "Don't Go to Business School," Squidoo, accessed on May 30, 2013 http://www.squidoo.com/Alternative-MBA.

[77] "Ya Es Oficial: Hay Muchos Más MBA de los Que Necesita Nuestra Sociedad" (It Is Official: There Are

227

Many More MBAs than Needed by Society"), *El Confidencial*, January 9, 2013.
[78] "MBA salary – enhancing power slashed", Financial Times, January 27, 2013, http://www.ft.com/intl/cms/s/2/e7e1e21a-6621-11e2-b967-00144feab49a.html#axzz2QwjqMsSw
[79] "2011 Application Trend Survey Report," Graduate Management Admission Council, http://www.gmac.com/market-intelligence-and-research/research-library/admissions-and-application-trends/2011-application-trends-survey-report.aspx.
[80] "Cost of MBA Teaches Tough Financial Lesson," ibid.
[81] www.qopolis.com
[82] Josh Kaufman, *The Personal MBA: A World-Class Business Education in a Single Volume*, ibid.
[83] Seth Godin, "Eleven Things Organizations Can Learn from Airports," Seth Godin's blog, January 27, 2013, accessed on May 30, 2013 http://sethgodin.typepad.com/seths_blog/2013/01/ten-things-organizations-can-learn-from-airports-.html.
[84] Philip Delves Broughton, *Ahead of the Curve*, ibid.
[85] Henry Mintzberg, ibid.
[86] "Chaud Business entre HEC et l'ESSEC" (Hot business between HEC and ESSEC), Liberation, May 14th 2004, accessed on May 30, 2013 http://www.liberation.fr/societe/0101488799-chaud-business-entre-hec-et-l-essec
[87] Ibid.
[88] "What if You Don't Want to Be a Manager?" *Harvard Business Review*, December 13, 2012,

Notes

http://blogs.hbr.org/cs/2012/12/what_if_you_dont_want_to_be_a.html.

[89] "For Newly Minted MBAs, a Smaller Paycheck Awaits," ibid.

[90] "Is the MBA Overrated?" ibid.

[91] John A. Byrne, "Why Josh Kaufman Thinks Business School Is a Waste," Poets & Quants, accessed on May 30, 2013 http://poetsandquants.com/2010/10/04/why-josh-kaufman-thinks-business-school-is-a-waste/.

[92] Keith Ferrazzi, *Never Eat Alone* (2005).

[93] This expression is the translation of the Spanish version of the book, so it is possible that the wording is not exact according to the original English version.

[94] "Think Twice," *The Economist*, January 2011, accessed on May 30, 2013 http://www.economist.com/whichmba/think-twice.

[95] Jeff Jarvis, *What Would Google Do?*, 2009.

[96] Dale Stephens, *Hacking your education Ditch the Lectures, Save thousands of dollars and learn more than your peers ever will*, 2013

[97] Napoleon Hill, ibid.

[98] Henry Mintzberg, ibid.

[99] "The End of Business Schools? Less Success than Meets the Eye," ibid.

[100] Ibid.

[101] "The End of Business Schools? Less Success than Meets the Eye," ibid.

[102] Henry Mintzberg, ibid.

[103] Josh Kaufman, *The Personal MBA: A World-Class Business Education in a Single Volume*, ibid.

[104] Josh Kaufman, Josh, "The Ninety-Nine Best Business Books," accessed May 21, 2013, http://personalmba.com/best-business-books/.
[105] Dale Stephens, *Hacking your education Ditch the Lectures, Save thousands of dollars and learn more than your peers ever will*, ibid.
[106] Sergio Fernandez, *Vivir sin Miedos (Living Without Fear)*, 2010.
[107] Jeff Jarvis, ibid.
[108] edX website, https://www.edx.org/.
[109] Coursera website, https://www.coursera.org/.
[110] "Business Schools Face a Challenging Future," *Financial Times*, January 7, 2013, http://www.ft.com/intl/cms/s/2/e111f93e-3a39-11e2-a00d-00144feabdc0.html#axzz2LLGNUiMJ.
[111] *Harvard Business Review* online store, http://hbr.org/store.
[112] La Vuelta al Mundo en Moto website, http://www.lavueltaalmundoenmoto.com/.
[113] Blaise Pascal (Clermont-Ferrand, June 19, 1623 – Paris, August 19, 1662) French mathematician, physicist, Christian philosopher, and writer.
[114] Daniel Goleman, *Emotional Intelligence* (1995).
[115] Philip Delves Broughton, *Ahead of the Curve*, ibid.
[116] StrengthsFinder, accessed on May 22, 2013, http://www.strengthsfinder.com/home.aspx.
[117] Philip Delves Broughton, *Ahead of the Curve*, ibid.
[118] Philip Delves Broughton, "Rewriting the HBS Mission Statement," July 13, 2009, Philip Delves Broughton's blog, http://philipdelvesbroughton.com/2009/07/13/rewriting-the-hbs-mission-statement/.

Notes

[119] Florence Noiville, ibid.
[120] Henry Mintzberg, ibid.
[121] Ibid.
[122] Eric Ries, *The Lean Startup*, 2011.
[123] Henry Mintzberg, ibid.
[124] "Las Profesiones en las Que Sólo Pueden Trabajar 'los Hijos de…'" ("Professions at Which only 'the Children of…' Can Be Employed"), *El Confidencial*, February 23, 2013, http://www.elconfidencial.com/alma-corazon-vida/2013/02/23/las-profesiones-en-las-que-solo-pueden-trabajar-los-hijos-de-115500/.
[125] Philip Delves Broughton, *Ahead of the Curve*, ibid.
[126] "Ne Vous Trompez Pas: Pourquoi un MBA n'est Pas Rentable," ibid.
[127] Olivier Roland's crazy side project, Personal MBA blog, January 2009, accessed 30 May 2013 http://personalmba.com/olivier-rolands-crazy-side-project/

Made in the USA
Lexington, KY
09 October 2015